CW00644365

BTEC FIRST SPORT

edexcel

BTEC
FIRST

> **Certificate**

> **Diploma**

SPORT

John
Honeybourne

Published in 2005 by:
Nelson Thornes Ltd
Delta Place
27 Bath Road
CHELTENHAM
GL53 7TH
United Kingdom

05 06 07 08 09 / 10 9 8 7 6 5 4 3 2 1

A catalogue record for this book is available from the British Library

ISBN 0 7487 8553 1

Illustrations by Oxford Designers and Illustrators and Peters & Zabransky Ltd
Page make-up by Florence Production Ltd

Printed in Great Britain by Scotprint

Contents

Acknowledgements

The publishers are indebted to the following for permission to reproduce copyright material:

- The British Canoe Union for reproduction of material from their web site (www.bcu.org.uk); Jonny Wilkinson/The Times/ NI Syndication for adapted newspaper article on page 135; The English Institute of Sport Ltd; The Science Museum; UEFA; CCPR; Youth Sport Trust and UK Sport.

Photographs

- Fig 1.1 Tennis net: Photodisc 10 (NT); Fig 1.2 Rugby/scoring a try: Photodisc 51 (NT); Fig 1.3 Girl watching TV in her room: AYA815 © copyright Simon Grosset/Alamy; Fig 1.4 Rock climber: Digital Vision XA (NT); Fig 1.5 Anna Kournikova: A2AD3E © copyright Alamy; Fig 1.6 Sport Outdoor Leisure Cycling: APCDDA © copyright Aflo Foto Agency/Alamy; Fig 1.8 Females/football: Corel 776 (NT); Fig 1.9 Determined Athlete: Photodisc 14b (NT); Fig 1.10 Black footballer: Photodisc 44 (NT); Fig 1.11 Ramblers/mountains: Photodisc 51 (NT); Fig 1.12 UK Sport emblem reproduced with permission; Fig 1.13 YST emblem reproduced with permission; Fig 1.14 UEFA emblem reproduced with permission; Fig 1.15 CCPR emblem reproduced with permission; Fig 1.16 Olympic flag: Corel 205 (NT); Fig 1.17 Sponsorship advertising on clothing: Corel 231 (NT); Fig 1.18 England fans queue at a turnstile at the City of Manchester stadium: AX2A19 © copyright Stephen Roberts/Alamy; Fig 1.19 Black male sprinter: Photodisc 10 (NT); Fig 1.20 A women's rugby game in action: AG8164 © copyright Stephen Voss/Alamy; Fig 1.21 Cricket/teenagers: Corel 685 (NT); Fig 1.22 Wales v Serbia and Montenegro Football Millennium Stadium: AM3855 © copyright The Photolibrary Wales/Alamy.
- Fig 2.1 Rugby scrum: Corel 745 (NT); Fig 2.2 Female athlete warming up: Photodisc 51 (NT); Fig 2.3 Athlete/drink: Photodisc 67 (NT); Fig 2.4 Canoeist in rough waters: Corel 451 (NT); Fig 2.5 Canoeist wearing safety equipment: Photodisc 51 (NT); Fig 2.7 Tennis player: Corel 578 (NT); Fig 2.8 Acupuncture: Photodisc 40 (NT); Fig 2.9 Yoga: Photodisc 67 (NT); Fig 2.10 Javelin: Corel 205 (NT); Fig 2.11 Squash Player/goggles: Photodisc 10 (NT).
- Fig 3.1 Weightlifter/female: Corel 423 (NT); Fig 3.2 Cricket bowler: Corel 778 (NT); Fig 3.3 Sprinter/blocks: Corel C772 (NT);

Fig 3.4 Handgrip dynamometer: Action Plus Sports Images; Fig 3.5 Sit-ups: Photodisc 51 (NT); Fig 3.6 The sit and reach test: FitnessASSIST, www.fitnessassist.co.uk, Tel: 01978 660077; Fig 3.7 Haile Gebrselassie (ABC162) © Copyright Alamy; Fig 3.8a Olympic male athlete: Photodisc 14b (NT); Fig 3.8b Bowls players: Corel 550 (NT); Fig 3.9a Marathon runner: Corel 337 (NT); Fig 3.9b High jumper: Corel 364 (NT); Fig 3.10 Male weightlifter: Corel 745 (NT); Fig 3.11 Swimmer: Digital Vision 11 (NT); Fig 3.12 Cross country runner: Photodisc 51 (NT); Fig 3.13 Male discus thrower: Photodisc 14b (NT); Fig 3.14 Long jumper: Corel 364 (NT); Fig 3.15 Burger café: Bananastock 50 (NT); Fig 3.16 A balanced diet © Crown copyright; Fig 3.18 Female discus thrower: Photodisc 14b (NT); Fig 3.19 Athlete under stress: Photodisc 14b (NT); Fig 3.22 Female hockey player: Corel 778 (NT);

- Fig 4.5 Female hockey player: Corel 205 (NT); Fig 4.7 Javelin/shoulder joint: Photodisc 14b (NT); Fig 4.10 Weightlifter: Corel 264 (NT); Fig 4.11 Gymnast – high bar extension: Corel 205 (NT); Fig 4.12 Gymnast – leg side extension: Photodisc 14b (NT); Fig 4.13 Man in pool (AH7891 L) Bildagentur Franz Waldhaeusl/Alamy; Fig 4.14 Cricket/teenagers: Corel 685 (NT); Fig 4.15 Ballet dancer: Digital Stock V75 (NT); Fig 4.16 Table tennis player: Corel 364 (NT); Fig 4.17 Discus thrower/back circle: Photodisc 14b (NT); Fig 4.18 Gymnast with pointed toes: Photodisc 14b (NT); Fig 4.19 Man swimming under water in pool (A4G642 L) Niall McOnegal/Alamy; Fig 4.21 Rugby tackle: Corel 745 (NT); Fig 4.22 Male sprinter: Corel 205 (NT); Fig 4.28 Long distance athletes: Corel 772 (NT);
- Fig 5.1 Clive Woodward (AG282D) © copyright Alamy; Fig 5.2 Interior of ambulance (AB322A) © copyright SHOUT/Alamy; Fig 5.3 Alex Ferguson (AADE10) © copyright Alamy; Fig 5.4 Sports coach: Corel 772 (NT); Fig 5.5 Child/bike stabilisers:Photodisc 38 (NT); Fig 5.6 Woman gymnast on balance beam (A0FE4C) © copyright Index Stock/Alamy.
- Fig 6.1 Hockey player/female: Corel 776 (NT); Fig 6.2 David Beckham (A0J12E) © copyright Alamy; Fig 6.3 Jonny Wilkinson (AG2970) © copyright Alamy; Fig 6.4 Golfer with crowd: Corel 665 (NT); Fig 6.5 Football/Goalkeeper: Digital Vision 12 (NT); Fig 6.6 Archer: Photodisc 10 (NT); Fig 6.7 Mark Lewis-Francis (ABC134) © copyright Alamy; Fig 6.8 Sportsperson preparing a healthy meal: Photodisc 67 (NT); Fig 6.9 Sports physiotherapist: Photodisc 40 (NT); Fig 6.10 Gail Devers (ABC072) © copyright Alamy.
- Fig 7.1 Checking CV: Photodisc 73 (NT); Fig 7.2 Interview: Photodisc 73 (NT); Fig 7.3 Sport Footabll Brazil Coach Luiz

Felipe Scolari (A283B5) © copyright POPPERFOTO/Alamy; Fig 7.4 Gym equipment: Photodisc 51 (NT).

- Fig 8.1 Football match: Corel 364 (NT); Fig 8.2 Golfer: Photodisc 51 (NT); Fig 8.3 Basketball: Photodisc 10 (NT); Fig 8.4 Demonstrating tennis serve: Corel 578 (NT); Fig 8.5 Netball team practising at secondary school UK (A9C024) © copyright Photofusion Picture Library/Alamy;
- Fig 8.6 Referee for ice hockey: Photodisc 10 (NT); Fig 8.7 Scoreboard (AYF849) © copyright Alamy; Fig 8.8 Track and field meet event starter (AJ7D5) © copyright Dennis MacDonald/Alamy; Fig 8.9 Football referee (A0J30A) © copyright POPPERFOTO/Alamy.

Dedication

I would like to thank my wife and family
for their support whilst writing this book.

Introduction

This book has been written predominantly as a student resource. All students and teachers of the BTEC First Diploma in Sport will find this an invaluable resource when completing their assignments in both the core and the optional units. Students following the BTEC First Certificate in Sport will also find this text useful because the same units make up the certificate, and therefore the same material is covered.

This book is written in a style that students will find easy to read and understand. Each chapter covers a different unit which makes up the qualification, and the learning outcomes match those stated in the examination board's specifications. The first three chapters (The sports industry; Health, safety and injury; and Preparation for sport) cover the first three compulsory core units of the qualification. The remaining chapters cover the optional units from which students must choose three to complete. A list of references and further reading will lead students to the additional knowledge and understanding necessary to fulfil the requirements of the qualification.

This book gives many practical examples and will help students to apply theoretical principles to real-life sports situations. Teachers in schools and colleges deliver the BTEC qualifications in a variety of different ways including direct teaching, student research, group work, practical work, work placement projects and personal sports performance.

Assessment includes the completion of assignments and external tests. The progress checks at the end of each chapter will help to reinforce learning and highlight the important aspects of each assignment for each unit.

Within the text there are definitions and 'In practice' examples to help students understand the many interesting but complex theoretical and practical aspects related to sport. Chapter 8 gives useful guidance to students in developing the practical sports skills needed for optional Unit 11 of the qualification – Practical Sport.

This book will be enjoyable for students to read as they progress through the qualification and will be one of the main resources for the course.

The sports industry

This chapter covers the essential theory for this Core Unit. The material in this chapter is central to the course and it will be useful to refer to this when studying other units. The chapter covers the nature of sport and what it means to our society, including who plays sport and who does not and why. The organisation and funding of sport in the UK is also discussed. There are important influences on sport in our society and this chapter covers the role of the media, professionalism and the misuse of drugs in sport.

Learning objectives

- To understand the nature of sport, participation of people in sports and sports development.

- To increase knowledge about the organisation of sport in the UK.

- To understand how sport is funded.

- To explore the main issues related to the influence of the media, professionalism and the use of drugs in sport.

1.1 The nature of sport

It is important to recognise what we mean by the term 'sport'.

Sport involves a competitive activity. Competition can be against individuals. For example: in skiing, individuals compete against each other; in the high-jump individuals try to jump higher than their competitors. Competitions can also be between teams, for example a hockey or football team playing against another team. Sport is frequently watched by people (spectators). The audience or spectators often pay to watch professional sport; for example, those who wish to watch county cricket have to pay to enter the ground.

> ### Definition
>
> **Sport**
>
> This involves competition between individuals or teams that is organised and includes physical activity.

▌▌▌*In Practice*

Competition
Both individual and team competitions can exist at the same time. For example, in rugby one prop forward competes against another

Figure 1.1 Sport involves an element of chance or luck

Invasion games

The object of this type of game is to invade the opponent's territory as if you were at war with the opposition – which of course you are not! Rugby, netball and football are examples of invasion games.

Target games

As the name suggests, the plan is to hit certain targets. This involves accuracy of judgement often called 'marksmanship'. Target games include golf and archery.

to push harder in the scrummage, but also the prop forward is part of the whole rugby team competing against the other team.

In most sports there is a winner and a loser, and in some cases you can have a draw where there is no clear winner. Sport involves a certain amount of luck or chance, for example, in tennis the ball may hit the net cord and travel over to the other side, thus winning a point. Sports also involve rules so that the competition is fair and there is no cheating or unfair advantage to a team or an individual. There is usually a defined place to play, for example a netball court or a football pitch. These sports places usually have boundaries, for example the sideline on a hockey pitch.

We use lots of different terms when describing activities related to sport. The following are often referred to as different types of sport:

- invasion games
- target games
- court games
- field sports.

In Practice

Amateurs and professionals

Sport can be played on an amateur or a professional basis. An example of an amateur sports person is a netball player who plays for her local club or a rugby player who plays for his local club. Neither of these players would receive any money for playing the

Figure 1.2 Invasion games involve invading the opponents' territory

Definition

Court games

These games include tennis, squash and volleyball. Usually there is no contact between the players and a net separates the court, although in squash both players occupy the same space.

Field sports

These are often associated with rural areas. Sports such as hunting, shooting and fishing are field sports and often involve killing animals (sometimes the prey becomes food for the hunter). However, the point of most field sports is the competition between man and the animal he wishes to kill.

Many people who participate in field sports describe the 'thrill of the chase' as the most enjoyable aspect of this type of sport. Others oppose this activity and view it as cruel and unsporting because the animal has no choice in its participation and it is not a fair competition.

sport. A professional might be a county cricket player or a football player who plays in the Nationwide League. Both of these people are paid to play sport – it is their job to play the sport and therefore they are called professional players. Some players are semi-professionals and they receive money for playing but do not earn enough to make a living from the sport; therefore they have other jobs from which they earn an income.

Leisure activities

This is a term that we use for many different activities, which may involve sport, but sport is different to leisure. Leisure is a wider term used to describe activities we are involved in that are nothing to do with work or home/family commitments such as cleaning your room. We choose to be involved in leisure, we do not have to do it. Leisure activities include watching TV, going to the cinema, skateboarding in the park or reading a book. Leisure time has increased over the last 100 years. Due to the invention of computers and machines that do many of our tasks, we now have much more time to spend on leisure activities.

People participate in leisure activities for a number of reasons, for example to escape the stresses of everyday life and to do something enjoyable. Some get involved in leisure activities in order to meet other people and make new friends.

Figure 1.3 Leisure involves activities that are nothing to do with work or other commitments

Recreation

Recreation is the term given for a more physically active aspect of leisure. Recreation is not curling up in front of the TV, it relates to doing something useful and constructive. For some people, recreation involves sports activities as well as cooking or gardening. For others, cooking and gardening would be viewed as anything but recreational! This is because some people see these activities as chores that are not particularly enjoyable. So recreation is related to a state of mind – it involves us viewing the activity not as work but as active enjoyment that helps us to relax and escape stress.

Outdoor and adventurous recreation activities involve individual challenge, for example climbing and canoeing.

Many adventurous recreation activities take place in the natural environment. There has been increased interest in outdoor and adventurous sports, and the term 'extreme sports' is used to describe sports which have elements of danger associated with them. Mountain biking, climbing, windsurfing and skateboarding are popular examples of these.

Lifetime sports

These are sports such as badminton and golf that can be carried on throughout our lives. When you get older, it does not mean you cannot be involved in such sports, thereby keeping fit, active and being socially involved with other people.

The leisure industry

The leisure industry has grown rapidly over the last 20 years. We now have more leisure time and are more willing to spend our money on leisure activities. The more money we are able to spend, the greater the growth of the industry in which we spend it. Hence the growth of the leisure industry. Sport is very commercialised and events and sports competitors are often sponsored for large sums of money.

In practice

The products associated with leisure include, for example, trainers and other sports clothing, DVDs and videos etc.

Leisure services include cinemas, sports stadia, skateboard parks and leisure centres.

Large multinational companies such as MGM often control the business of leisure.

Leisure centres and health clubs

There has been huge growth in the number of health clubs and leisure centres both in the private sector (owned by commercial companies) and in the public sector (run by local councils and

Figure 1.4 Adventurous recreation involves personal challenge

Definition

Definition

The leisure industry
The products and services associated with leisure activities.

subsidised by the taxpayer). The private and public sectors are explored in more detail later in the chapter.

Private clubs have seen massive growth over the last five years, for example Livingwell, LA Fitness, Fitness First and the David Lloyd Centres. There is also demand for private trainers who are fitness professionals who work with individuals for an hourly fee. Other services have also benefited from this health and fitness boom, for example nutrition advice and beauty treatment.

▌▌▌ *In practice*

The LA Fitness health clubs are in the private sector. People pay a membership fee, usually for the year, and in return they get access to the club's health and fitness facilities.

Local leisure centres are in the public sector and are part funded by the taxpayer. They also charge for the use of their facilities but the fees are not as expensive as the private health clubs.

Sports clothing and equipment

Along with this massive rise of interest in the health and fitness industry, clothing and equipment requirements have also increased. Sports clothing has become highly fashionable and even those who do not participate in any sport often spend money on sports clothing in order to keep up with fashion.

There is now greater competition between sports equipment manufacturers to gain more sales, for example to sell the latest training shoes or the high-spec tennis rackets. There is also a big market for fitness equipment for the home, for example Boots now sell punch bags, exercise machines and yoga mats!

1.2 Sports participation

There are many ways in which people are influenced to either participate in or watch sport. There are those who show no interest in sports whatsoever, but even they may wish to stay healthy and may well do some exercise or consider their diet carefully.

There is still a difference between the participation levels of men and women in sport. Far more men get involved in sport either to participate or to spectate. Some people still think that being good at sport or interested in sport is unfeminine, thus reinforcing male dominance in sport and sport coverage.

▌▌▌ *In practice*

In tennis there is a huge discrepancy in prize money, with women getting far less than men. A lot of the media interest in women tennis players focuses on their looks.

Figure 1.5 The media often focus on the looks of female players rather than their sporting abilities

Of course there are many positive aspects of female sport. More women are now involved in physical exercise and there is far more interest in health and fitness matters. The participation rates for women involved in sports such as football and rugby are now much larger and continue to grow.

The reasons that people get involved in sport include:

* Benefits to health and fitness – sport can make us fitter and therefore healthier.
* Greater sense of well-being. Many people report that they feel better after participating in sport. It is accepted that certain hormones are released during exercise and that these can help us to feel more optimistic about life and better about ourselves.
* To combat stress. Many people often use sport as an escape from their working life. It has been recognised that by playing sport we can release some of our pent-up frustrations and aggressions, for example, hitting the squash ball hard to get rid of anger caused by frustrations at work or at college.
* The benefits of learning new skills. Gaining a sense of accomplishment and also eventually being able to compete at a higher level and increasing our self-satisfaction when we overcome challenges and barriers.
* Meeting and participating with other people. It is possible to make new friends through sport and that is important for our sense of well-being.

Figure 1.6 Sport can help people to make new friends

In practice

The London Marathon

An event with mixed participation that combines seriously competitive runners, those who are looking for a personal challenge and those who are running to make money for charity. More than 33 000 runners took part in the twenty-fourth London Marathon in April 2004. The event doubled as the British Olympic trials, and in order to qualify for Athens runners needed to record a time below 2 hours 15 minutes for the men and 2 hours 37 minutes for the women.

One of the most important benefits of sport is that it is hugely enjoyable and many of us seek competition that is fair and tests our own capabilities.

The reasons that many do not get involved in sport include:

- Time – work commitments can get in the way of participating in sport.
- Resources – there may not be appropriate facilities or sports clubs nearby and this can dictate whether or not people participate in sport. Some local authorities lay on transport for those who wish to visit a sports facility, for example the elderly may catch a specially run bus to a local leisure centre.

In practice

The benefits of sport – some facts

Reports commissioned by Sport England suggest that sport is helping to get youngsters away from crime and assisting in the fight against drug abuse.

In Bristol there has been a 40% reduction in crime levels on the Southmead Estate since the first sport development worker was appointed.

1.3 Sports development

UK Sport, formally called the Sports Council, produced a report called 'Better Quality Sport for All'. This report highlighted the need to enable people to learn basic sports skills that can be built upon to achieve sporting excellence. The report listed the following aims:

- To develop the skills and competence to enable sport to be enjoyed.
- For all to follow a lifestyle which includes active participation in sport and recreation.
- For people to achieve their personal goals at their chosen level of involvement in sport.
- For developing excellence and for achieving success in sport at the highest level.

(Adapted from Sport England web site, 2000)

The report stated that everyone has the right to play sport. Whether it is for fun, for health, to enjoy the natural environment or to win, everyone should have the opportunity to enjoy sport. The challenge was to make 'England the sporting nation'.

The sport development continuum

This was originally called the 'pyramid of participation' and was developed into the continuum when it was recognised that most adults do not participate in sport. This non-participation has stemmed from a non-active lifestyle and the fact that many people are put off sport as a result of school PE experiences.

A new strategy was developed following the 'Better Quality Sport for All' report (UK Sport web site, 1996). This included:

- working with schools to encourage children to become active sporting adults.
- working with non-participating adults to encourage them to take up sport.

The continuum is shown in Figure 1.7.

1 Foundation – this stage concerns the development of basic skills in sport. Good exercise habits combined with appropriate knowledge and understanding help in the development of positive attitudes to sport.

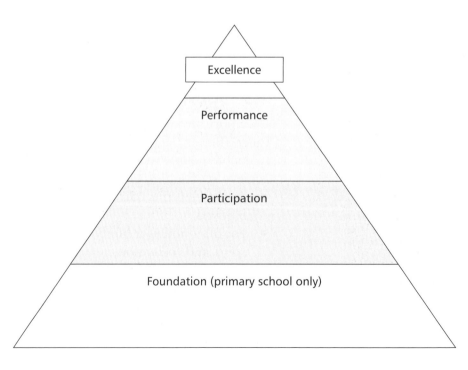

Figure 1.7 Sport development continuum model

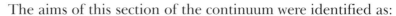

Figure 1.8 There is a need to generate more positive attitudes to sport, especially amongst girls

The aims of this section of the continuum were identified as:
(a) To increase curriculum time for PE in schools.
(b) To increase the number of children taking part in extracurricular sport.
(c) To increase the percentage of children taking part in out-of-school sport.
(d) To generate more positive attitudes to sport, especially by girls, that is to increase the percentage of young people taking part in a range of sports on a 'regular' basis.

2   Participation – this stage is concerned with getting as many people involved in sport as possible:

The aims of this section of the continuum were:
(a) To increase the number of people taking part in regular sporting activity.
(b) To reduce the number of people who drop out of sport as they get older.
(c) To reduce barriers to participation in sport.

3   Performance – this concerns the improvement of coaching standards. It relates to competitive sport and seeks to encourage people to obtain fulfilment by improving their performance.

The aims related to this section of the continuum are:
(a) To increase the numbers of participants who are trying to improve their sporting skills.
(b) To increase the number of sports club members.

4   Excellence – this stage is concerned with reaching the top standards in sport, such as national and international competition.

The aims of this section of the continuum are:
(a) To achieve improved levels of performance in terms of world rankings, record wins and losses, national and international records and individual personal bests.
(b) For UK teams to achieve success in international competition.

Target groups

Target groups are often identified and particular strategies put in place to ensure that everyone in society has an equal chance to get involved in sport. UK sports organisations have identified particular groups of people whose participation rates in sport are below those of other groups.

Figure 1.9 The 'Excellence' stage is concerned with individual personal bests

Definition

Participation rates

This refers to the number of people within a group who are involved in sport compared with those who are not. For example, in a school the participation rates for girls in extra-curricular sport could be 30%. In other words, three out of every 10 girls in the school are regular members of a sports team or club.

Sports' equity

This concerns fairness in sport, equality of access, recognising inequalities and taking steps to address them. It is about changing the culture and structure of sport to ensure that it becomes equally accessible to all members of society, whatever their age, ability, gender, race, ethnicity, sexuality or social/economic status. Sports equity, then, is more concerned with the sport itself. (Sport England web site, 2002)

There are many examples of inequality in sport. The following are generally recognised as being groups of people who are not getting a fair chance in sport:

- ethnic minority communities
- people with disabilities
- women
- the over-50 age group.

However, these are not the only people who are not getting fair access to sport.

Equity concerns fairness and access for all. In sport, as in life, there are many individuals and groups who may feel discriminated against.

UK Sport has a written statement regarding equity in sport, as follows:

Equity

Equity is about recognising and removing the barriers faced by people involved, or wanting to be involved in sport. It is about changing the culture of sport to one that values diversity and enables the full involvement of disadvantaged groups in every aspect of sport.

UK Sport equality statement

UK Sport recognises that discrimination is unacceptable and will not tolerate discrimination on the grounds of race, special needs, including learning and physical disabilities, class or social background, religion, sexual orientation, ethnic or national origins, gender, marital status, pregnancy, age, colour or political persuasion.

UK Sport will take positive action to eliminate individual and institutional discrimination; to comply with its statutory and legislative obligations; to meet the needs of its staff and partners and to make equality and equal treatment a core issue in the development, delivery and refinement of our policies, initiatives and services and in the way we manage our staff.

UK Sport is committed to achieving equality in sport and is taking a proactive approach in this area. It is central to the Modernisation Programme and progressive, dynamic sports organisations are those that can demonstrate effective equality strategies and programmes.

To underline our commitment, UK Sport:

- has developed an Equality Strategy and Race Equality Scheme that will ensure we meet our legal obligations as well as establishing equality principles and policies within UK Sport and our work with partner organisations

- has appointed an Equity Co-ordinator to support the organisation and its partners in developing and implementing equality strategies and programmes
- will seek to collate and disseminate good practice from across the UK, including the work of Home Country Sports Councils and equity organisations
- developed the Equality Standard for sport for governing bodies and sports organisations
- co-ordinated the development of the UK Strategy Framework for Women and Sport
- will continue to represent the UK in equality issues and good practice to the international sport and equality movement
- is working with disability sports organisations to develop appropriate processes for drug-testing.

(UK Sport web site, 2004)

Barriers to participation

There are still examples and practices that go against the sense of sports equity or fairness of opportunity that has been described above.

▌▌▌*In practice*

'Kick racism out of football'

This was a slogan adopted by a campaign started in 1993 to cut racial harassment in football by fans and by players. The Commission for Racial Equality and the Professional Footballers Association both backed the campaign.

There are also financial barriers to participation in many sports. Some sports are beyond the reach of people because they cannot afford the equipment, facilities or membership fees to participate. Work and family commitments may also make it difficult for people to be involved in sport.

Influences of sports development

The sports development policies of local authorities include a variety of methods to promote and develop sport at all points of the continuum. Local authorities will support schools and colleges with help and advice from sports development officers. (The role of local authorities is explored later in this chapter.)

▌▌▌*In practice*

Sports development officers

These can be experts in a particular sport who have sports skills and also coaching expertise. They include general officers who deal with a variety of sports and activities within a particular target group and also specific sport officers who concentrate on increasing participation in one specific sport.

Figure 1.10 'Kick racism out of football' is a campaign to cut racial harassment

1.4 Organisation of sport

Organisations that are associated with sport in the UK can be divided into three groups: **public, private and voluntary**. We all pay taxes to the government who in turn fund the public organisations (funding is dealt with later in this chapter). The private-sector organisations include commercial businesses trying to make a profit and non-profit making voluntary organisations such as the Youth Hostels Association or amateur sports clubs.

▌*In practice*

If in order to keep fit you want to find appropriate facilities to train and exercise then you could use public, private or voluntary facilities.

- *Public facilities include your local leisure centre, run by the local authority and funded via the taxpayer.*
- *Private facilities include the local private health and fitness club.*
- *The voluntary sector facilities include the local athletic club where you could train to keep fit. Another example is the Youth Hostels Association, which would give you information and concessionary rates to stay at youth hostels so that you can walk or ramble to keep fit.*

The public sector includes local authorities and their sports development officers. The local authorities promote sport according to their own local needs, for example to promote basketball in order to improve levels of participation and excellence.

The private sector also provides sport according to local needs and often strives to get as many people involved as possible, to raise attendance levels and, most importantly because they are money-making organisations, to improve their profits. One example of a private club is LA Fitness health and fitness club, which provides equipment, instruction in fitness activities and also personal training.

The voluntary sector aims to provide support for local needs. Voluntary organisations may promote specific sports, for example the local hockey club, which will strive to get as many people to play hockey as possible and to attract men and women from all walks of life. Such a club will run teams in local leagues and hold training sessions for their members.

Other agencies are as follows.

Skill Active

This is the national training organisation for sport and recreation. It offers training for leisure attractions, health and fitness instructors, outdoor activities, the caravan industry, playwork with children as well as sport and recreation.

Figure 1.11 Sport is provided through public, private and voluntary means

Department for Culture, Media and Sport (DCMS)

This government department is responsible for government policy related to sport. A minister associated with the department is responsible for sport.

In the year 2000/01, for instance, the budget for the department was approximately £1 billion, 90% of which went directly to service providers in cultural and sporting sectors.

The budget is forecast to be approximately £1.6 billion by 2005/06. This includes £25 million for coaching; £6 million for talent scholarships; £20 million per year for facilities at Community Amateur Sports Clubs. There is also a guarantee to maintain levels of funding through the World Class Performance Programme. (Central Council for Physical Recreation (CCPR) web site, 2002)

For more information see www.culture.gov.uk.

Figure 1.12
UK Sport emblem

UK Sport

In 1972 the national sports councils were formed and these were independent of the government. In 1996 there was a reorganisation of the Sports Councils and UK Sport (sometimes called the UK Sports Council) was formed.

UK Sport is an agency under government direction to provide support for elite sportspeople who have a high level of performance or have the potential to reach the top. The organisation distributes government funds including lottery money. It also supports world-class performers and promotes ethical standards of behaviour; its anti-doping programme aims to fight the use of performance-enhancing drugs.

UK Sport works in partnership with each of the home country sports councils. These are:

- Sport England.
- Sportscotland.
- Sports Council for Northern Ireland.
- Sports Council for Wales.
  For more information email info@uksport.gov.uk.

▌In practice

UK Sport works in partnership with the home countries and other agencies to drive the development of a world-class high-performance system in the UK. This will result in more winning athletes and greater world-class success.

UK Sport is responsible for managing and distributing public investment (£29 million annually) and is a statutory distributor of funds raised by the National Lottery (9.2% of sport allocation).

UK Sport is in a unique position to enhance and add value to the work of its partners through delivering on its primary and supporting goals:

Primary goal: World Class Performance
UK Sport works with its partners to help ensure that Britain's Olympic and Paralympic athletes have all the support they need to compete and win at the highest level. A network of scientific, medical, technical and coaching expertise is being developed to maximise medal potential.

Supporting goal: Worldwide Impact
The 2012 Olympic bid places UK Sport's international work in the spotlight. The UK's influence as an authoritative and leading player needs to be strengthened. UK Sport supports the bidding for and staging of major sporting events in the UK, and helps build relationships with key international partners to maintain the UK's standing in world sport.

Supporting goal: World Class Standards
UK Sport promotes the highest standards of sporting conduct and explores its wider social applications. It leads a world-class anti-doping programme for the UK and is responsible for improving the education and promotion of ethically fair and drug-free sport.

Youth Sport Trust

The Youth Sport Trust is a registered charity, established in 1994, which supports the education and development of all young people through physical education and sport.

The Trust has developed a series of linked and progressive PE and sport schemes for young people aged 18 months to 18 years called the TOP programmes. Their defining features are top quality resources, equipment and training and they are all accessible to young disabled people. For more information, please visit www.youthsporttrust.org

Governing bodies

The majority of sports that we know today were developed and organised in the late 19th century. The participants needed to agree rules and regulations for their sports and so they met and formed their own committees called governing bodies, for example the Football Association (FA), Lawn Tennis Association (LTA), Amateur Swimming Association (ASA), Rugby Football Union (RFU) etc. There are over 265 governing bodies in the UK. The teams and clubs pay a subscription to the governing body who, in turn, administer the sport nationally and organise competitions and the national team. There are still many voluntary positions within each governing body, but more salaried members of staff are now involved.

Definition

TOP Play and TOP Sport

TOP Play and TOP Sport are programmes that were jointly developed by the Youth Sport Trust, Sport England, the Physical Education profession and National Governing Bodies of Sport. The programmes are designed to support teachers, leaders, coaches and other adults in introducing young people to physical activity and sport through a series of fun games and activites

YOUTH SPORT TRUST

Figure 1.13 YST emblem

Figure 1.14 UEFA emblem

Figure 1.15 CCPR symbol

Figure 1.16 Olympic flag

The national governing bodies are also members of international governing bodies, for example Union des Associations Europeennes de Football (UEFA) and Fédération Internationale de Football Association (FIFA). These international bodies control and organise international competitions.

Central Council of Physical Recreation (CCPR)

The aim of the CCPR is to promote, protect and develop the interests of sport and physical recreation. This organisation is completely independent from government control and has no responsibility for allocating funds.

British Olympic Association (BOA)

The BOA was formed in 1905. Great Britain is one of only five countries that have never failed to be represented at the Olympics (since 1896!). The BOA supplies the delegates for the National Olympic Committee (NOC). Amongst other things the BOA is responsible for the planning and execution of the Great Britain Olympic Team's participation in the Olympic and Olympic Winter Games.

For more information see www.olympics.org.uk.

International Olympic Committee (IOC)

The IOC was created by the Paris Congress in 1894. It owns all of the rights to the Olympic symbol and the Games themselves. This is the world body that administers the Olympic Movement. Its headquarters are in Lausanne, Switzerland. Members are appointed to the IOC and are responsible for selecting the host cities of the Olympic Games, both summer and winter.

English Federation for Disability Sport (EFDS)

This is a national body that is responsible for developing sport for people with disabilities in England. They work closely with other national disability organisations recognised by Sport England:

- British Amputees and Les Autres Sports Association.
- British Blind Sport.
- British Deaf Sports Council.
- British Wheelchair Sports Foundation.
- Cerebral Palsy Sport.
- Disability Sport England.

1.5 Sources of funding in sport

Sports organisations have a number of different sources of funding.

Grants

These are usually made available to public and voluntary sectors and are granted by the government – both local and national – and the

European Union. However, increasingly, private-sector projects are being funded as long as the project benefits the local population. Buildings and equipment are typically funded by private-sector bodies. Many grants involve the sports organisation putting forward a percentage of the funds themselves, for example 50% of the costs are government funds and 50% are funded by the organisation.

Subsidies

If local authorities or councils tried to cover all of the costs of sport, few people would be able to participate, for example, in swimming. Therefore there is a system of subsidies whereby members of the public pay a certain amount and the local authority pays the rest. Taxpayers fund these subsidies via local government.

Membership fees

All sports organisations that have a membership can make a significant proportion of their income from membership fees. For example, to join a hockey club an annual membership fee is paid by each player and often there is also a match fee paid by the player for each game that he or she plays.

The National Lottery

This provides a substantial grant for sport. The relatively newly formed (2002) English Institute of Sport to support world-class performers is also funded through the lottery. UK Sport is lottery funded and this in turn funds high-performance sport in the UK. Sport England, Sport Scotland and Sport Wales also receive lottery funds and these are used to support sport at all levels.

Sponsorship

The influence of sponsorship on the development of sport has been enormous. Sport is now big business, with large amounts of money being spent by commercial companies on sports participants and events. For example, a company such as Adidas might sponsor a top-class tennis player to wear a particular style of their training shoe. At the other end of the scale, a local hockey club may attract a small amount of sponsorship to go towards the first-team kit.

There has also been a significant increase in sponsorship due to sports clothing being fashionable. For instance there has been a huge increase in the sale of training shoes. Many of the people who wear trainers would never dream of participating in sport! Nevertheless commercial companies recognise that top sports stars can be fashion role models for the young and therefore use them in advertising campaigns.

Figure 1.17 Sponsors advertise on team clothing

▌▌ *In Practice*

British Olympic Association

The British Olympic Association (BOA) has announced Easynet as its Official Broadband Network Partner. Easynet will support the BOA for the next three years, throughout the Olympic Games in Athens 2004 and the Winter Olympics in Turin in 2006. Simon Clegg, Chief Executive of the BOA, has said:

> *'The BOA provides the infrastructure that enables elite British athletes to compete at the highest level. Easynet provides the infrastructure that will enable British business to compete in the global marketplace of the future. Easynet's sponsorship is a great example of British business getting behind British sport, and they will be joining our Olympic family which includes Adidas, Rover and Heineken.'*

Easynet is also supporting the BOA's Schools Programme which, as part of the National Curriculum, aims to raise awareness of the Olympics.

For more information see www.olympics.org.uk.
(Adapted from UK Sport web site, 2004)

According to independent research commissioned by the Sports Sponsorship Advisory Service, sports sponsorship is increasingly difficult to find for the middle-ranking sports.

A recent report – presented to national governing bodies at a seminar at the offices of the Central Council of Physical Recreation in 2002 – blames the lack of sponsorship on sports' inability to attract sufficient media coverage.

'Sports sponsorship can be a vital ingredient of the financing of governing bodies' activities', explained Howard Wells, Chairman of the CCPR.

'Many sports, however, are unable to attract sponsors because they cannot get television coverage. Sport must also begin to understand the value of its intellectual property rights and how best to market them in a rapidly changing market place.'

The main points in the report are:

1   Sponsors continue to seek image enhancement and brand awareness through sponsorship and see this as being largely dependent on broadcast and other media coverage.

2   Sponsors are also looking to sell their products, develop promotional opportunities and demonstrate that they are good corporate citizens.

3 Sponsors continue to be attracted to the top ten sports and/or to community-based activity, and middle-ranking sports are rarely considered.

4 Women's sport has the potential to attract more sponsors but to date most of this potential is unfulfilled.

5 Many sports are becoming more commercially aware but some demonstrate naïvety over valuing their rights and approaching sponsors.

'The current market place is difficult in particular for middle-ranking sports and even greater efforts are needed to develop their true potential', added Mike Reynolds, Director of the Institute of Sports Sponsorship. 'This is an increasingly competitive market and some sports have to become smarter and more professional.'

(Adapted from UK Sport web site, 2002)

Charging for products and services

Sports organisations charge for playing, for coaching and for spectating. The amount that is charged is often related to how popular the sport is, especially in the case of spectating.

Figure 1.18 Professional sport is heavily reliant upon entrance charging

Income from the mass media

The mass media provides a huge income for professional sport in the UK. Media includes satellite and terrestrial television companies and radio stations.

1.6 Key issues and the influence of the media on sport

Barriers to access

Some of the key issues in sports participation and development are related to barriers to access, in other words: what stops people being involved in sport. Here are some of the barriers and issues related to them:

- Social inclusion – this phrase relates to the need for everyone to have equal opportunities to take part in sport whatever their background or social standing.
- Racism – most sports are determined to stamp out any racist activities, for example the exclusion of black participants from their clubs. Racism involves discriminating against someone or acting against their best interests because of their racial background.

Figure 1.19 Most sports are determined to stamp out racism

- Sexism – this is discrimination against a person because of their gender, for example denying females equal playing rights in a golf club.
- Ageism – this is discrimination against someone because of their age, for example a health club failing to put on activities or classes suitable for their older clientele.

Figure 1.20 Social inclusion means the need for everyone to have an equal opportunity to take part in sport

▌▌ *In practice*

The growth of sports facilities has increased access, but even though there are more low-cost courses available, affordability is still a problem in sport. For many the most important questions relating to access are:

- *What is available?*
- *What is affordable?*
- *How do I feel about myself?*

This is sometimes identified by the three words: **provision**; **opportunity**; **esteem**.

The following are the main issues relating to access:

- **Opening times**, e.g. these may not be convenient for shift workers.
- **Age**, e.g. sport is often perceived as a young person's activity and the elderly may feel undignified if they participate in sport.
- **Race**, e.g. experiencing racial discrimination may be one reason for a lack of confidence to get involved in a predominantly white environment such as a golf club.

▌▌ *In practice*

People on low incomes living in a disadvantaged community in the north of England demonstrate some of the lowest levels of participation in sport ever measured.

(Headline from The Player, Sport England, Summer 2002)

- 71% of the British population take part in at least one sport, but in Liverpool the figure is only 51%.
- In Bradford the proportion of children swimming, cycling or walking is less than half the national average.
- 43% of British children play cricket; in Liverpool this percentage is only 3%.
- However, in Liverpool and Bradford the vast majority of children have a very positive view about the value of sport.

Figure 1.21 Only 3% of children in Liverpool play cricket

Drugs in sport

There is a lot of pressure on sports performers to win, sometimes at any cost, including risking personal harm, an outright ban and public humiliation. These are the risks associated with the use of drugs and banned substances which help sports performers do even better. Many elite sportspeople have tested positive for banned substances – some by accident, for example as a result of taking what was thought to be a 'safe' product, for example a cold remedy, and some because they wished to cheat. There are regular checks by governing sports' bodies, but the availability and use of performance-enhancing drugs has increased. The main categories of drugs used to enhance performance illegally are:

- Anabolic steroids – these enable the athlete to train harder and longer and increase strength and aggression.
- Amphetamines – a brain stimulant that increases alertness.

- Narcotic analgesics – these enable athletes to work harder and longer and they dull the pain of training or injury.
- Beta blockers – these help to control the heart rate and keep the athlete calm.
- Diuretics – these are taken by athletes to control or lose weight.

There are also sports performers who have taken illegal recreational drugs such as cocaine.

Influences of the media

Television companies spend an enormous amount of money on the broadcasting rights to sports events. To view certain events such as boxing matches the subscriber often has to pay extra (pay-per-view). For example, Sky holds the rights to many Premiership football games, which can only be viewed by subscribing to a Sky package.

Digital TV has also influenced sport and not always to everyone's benefit. The collapse of ITV Digital in 2002 meant that many football teams faced financial disaster, having been promised a considerable amount of money that never materialised.

The terrestrial channels such as BBC and ITV have lost many of the major sports events. The situation now arises, for example, where BBC news is unable to show clips of certain sporting events because the rights are owned by another company. Never before has so much sport been shown on TV, but because satellite TV dominates this coverage, only those who can afford to subscribe have access to many sports events. The range of sport shown is limited and football gets the most coverage. Male sport still dominates although there is refreshing interest in women's football for instance.

The rules of sport have been influenced by the media as has event programming because of the needs of the TV companies. For instance, football fans may find that their team is playing on a Sunday at 6.00 pm, which has not traditionally been a timeslot for the game. Olympic Games events are often scheduled at unsuitable times because of the demands of TV companies who are beaming the event around the world across different time zones. Rules have been affected. For instance, in cricket the third umpire in the form of video replay analysis has come into force largely due to the influence of TV. There has been a similar development in rugby football. The armchair spectator can now see the event at every angle and the officials' decisions are laid bare for scrutiny. Hence the need for new technology to aid the decision makers on the field of play.

Figure 1.22 Advertising revenue is a significant source of income

The extent of media involvement has also influenced the amount of sponsorship and advertising revenue available to participants, clubs and other sports organisations.

This has brought much welcomed money into sport, but some may argue that this has only been available to a small number of participants in a few sports and it may well have led to the decrease in participation in minority sports.

The media can encourage participation in sport. You only have to see the increased activity on municipal tennis courts during the Wimbledon fortnight to appreciate that watching sport can stimulate participation.

Our interest in playing a sport is particularly increased when the media highlights the success of UK sports performers. There was a surge of interest in curling, for instance, after success in the Winter Olympics.

The types of media involved in sport include:
* Television – BBC, ITV, Channel 4, Channel 5, satellite, cable, digital, factual/fiction/advertising.
* Press – broadsheets, tabloids, local, weekly, magazines, periodicals.
* The radio – national, local, commercial.
* Cinema – documentaries, movies (USA/UK/Bollywood and so on).

Progress check

1 What are the main differences between sport and recreation? Give examples.
2 Give examples of amateur and professional sports.
3 Why are sports like badminton and golf called 'lifetime sports'?
4 Give some of the possible reasons for people participating in the London Marathon.
5 Give examples of sports provision in the public, private and voluntary sectors.
6 Describe the activities of one of the following organisations: UEFA, Youth Sports Trust, Central Council for Physical Recreation, SPRITO.
7 Describe the different types of funding available for sport in the UK.
8 What are the benefits and drawbacks of sponsorship in sport?
9 What is meant by racism, sexism and ageism in sport? Give examples.
10 What are the advantages and disadvantages of the influence of the media on sport?

2

Health, safety and injury

This chapter covers the theoretical elements related to health, safety and injury for this Core Unit. Unit 2 has close links with many other units in this qualification. Other chapters refer back to the material here. This chapter investigates the major risk factors that can affect sportsmen and sportswomen in different sports settings. The causes of injury are covered together with measures to prevent injury in sport. The importance of recognising situations that require immediate expert advice will also be emphasised. This chapter also highlights the main relevant laws and regulations that deal with health and safety. In addition, there is useful material to support your own risk assessment of a given sports activity.

Learning objectives

- To understand the main risk factors that can cause sports injuries.

- To identify ways of minimising and preventing sports injuries.

- To increase knowledge related to health and safety rules and regulations.

- To increase knowledge of common sports injuries and basic treatment procedures.

- To be able to prepare a risk assessment for a sports activity.

2.1 The main risk factors in sport

The main risks for participants in sport are as follows.

Poor physical fitness/inappropriate physique for the activity

Sports activities require the participant to have at least some level of fitness. For example, to be involved in gymnastics you need to have some flexibility and the ability to support your own weight. A netball player needs to have some stamina and the ability to run up and down a netball court. If you wish to play rugby football as a forward

Figure 2.1 A rugby scrum

you will need to be physically strong in order to withstand the physical demands of scrummaging and to prevent the risk of injury.

Most sports are quite physically demanding and anyone who has an injury or health problems should seek advice from a qualified medical practitioner before participating.

Poor level of skill or technique

Many injuries are caused through inexperience. Some players new to sport will not know how to participate safely. For example, most injuries sustained in hockey at lower-ability levels are caused by inappropriate use of the hockey stick – a novice player does not have the stick control of a more experienced player. Club squash players have more eye injuries than international players because the ball is more likely to be struck in an inappropriate or unpredictable manner. Sports performers also sustain injuries because of poor technique. A golfer who has an inefficient golf swing can sustain back injuries. A tennis player who uses the wrist too much in shots may suffer wrist sprains. A javelin thrower who has an incorrect throwing technique can suffer arm, leg and back strains.

Lack of effective preparation for sport

It is crucial that all sports performers take appropriate steps before and after vigorous activity. This involves an effective warm-up and a cool-down following the activity, and it applies to all sports activities at all levels – even beginners need to warm up properly. The benefits of an effective warm-up and cool-down are well documented.

Figure 2.2 An effective warm-up is essential in order to prevent injury

The warm-up enables the body to prepare for exercise. It reduces the likelihood of injuries and muscle soreness. There is also a release of adrenaline and this will start to speed up the delivery of oxygen to the working muscles. Muscle temperature will increase, and that will help with the supply of much-needed energy. The muscle also becomes more flexible and this helps to prevent injury.

The cool-down is also important for effective training. If light exercise follows training, then the oxygen can be flushed through the muscle tissue more effectively and will oxidise lactic acid which needs to be dispersed in order to reduce muscle stiffness. Cool-downs also prevent blood pooling in the veins which can cause dizziness.

Dangerous training practices

There are many different training methods and some of the more conventional ones will be dealt with later in this book. However, there are some methods, not recognised by sports professionals, which may prove to be dangerous and cause injury or illness. Some types of training are suited only to the very best performers whose bodies are able to take, and indeed need, the extra stresses and strains in order to prepare for top competition. If a novice performer attempts advanced training methods then injury is much more likely. Training methods are dealt with in Chapters 3 and 6, but it is important that whatever the method of training certain safety issues are addressed. Health and safety is very important at all levels of sport.

In practice

Dangerous training practices
Serious injuries and even deaths have occurred during javelin training. Long-distance runners who have not prepared properly have suffered from severe heat exhaustion. Even very simple activities such as shooting at goal in hockey can be dangerous if safety is not emphasised; players should wait for the appropriate moment to shoot. In gymnastics horrendous spinal injuries have been caused as a result of pushing young gymnasts too far and getting them to attempt moves that they are not ready for – with disastrous consequences.

Inadequate or inappropriate diet

It is very important that a sports performer eats and drinks appropriately. Nutrition and sport is dealt with in detail in Chapter 3.

Food is neither healthy nor unhealthy – there are only bad uses of food. In other words, a balanced diet is required for good health and fitness. The intake of water before, during and after exercise is very important in order to avoid dehydration.

In practice

Studies show that individuals who are dehydrated become ill. The body's systems become inefficient if there is dehydration. When dehydrated the body cannot provide adequate blood flow to the skin and this is essential in order to get rid of unwanted heat. If the body remains hot then heat exhaustion is likely. Fluids must be consumed during prolonged exercise. This will make dehydration less likely and will slow the rise in body temperature.

Figure 2.3 Water is the most important constituent in any drink taken before, during and after exercise

Water is the most important constituent in any drink taken before, during and after exercise because it empties from the stomach extremely quickly and reduces dehydration associated with sweating.

Influence of alcohol or drugs

There are proven links between excessive consumption of alcohol and drugs, and illness. Sports people cannot afford to drink more alcohol than is advised (see Health Development Agency recommendations below).

In practice

The Health Development Agency recommend for adults:
- *Males: 3–4 units per day.*
- *Females: 2–3 units per day.*

One unit is equal to:

Half a pint 'ordinary strength' beer = 3.0–3.5% alcohol = 90 calories

OR

1 standard glass of wine = 11% alcohol = 90 calories

OR

A single measure of spirits = 38% alcohol = 50 calories.

Binge drinking is particularly bad for you, and this is a growing habit amongst teenagers and young adults. It is better to spread your alcohol consumption across the week and to leave some alcohol-free days.

More sportspeople are testing positive for drugs. This may indicate an increase in drug taking or that the drug testers are getting better at their job! Many performance-enhancing drugs have side effects that may seriously damage the health of the athlete.

In practice

Anabolic steroids

These are man-made drugs that increase muscle growth if taken during a regime of vigorous training. They also enable the athlete to recover more quickly and therefore to train even harder. The main problems with taking such drugs include the following:

- *both the liver and kidneys can develop tumours*
- *the liver ceases to act properly, causing major health problems*
- *high blood pressure*
- *severe acne or spots*
- *shrinking of the testicles, reduced sperm count and the development of breasts in males*
- *the growth of facial hair, baldness and deepening of the voice in females*
- *an increase in aggression and other psychological problems.*

Dangerous environment, for example broken bottles on a playing field

The playing field, court or track can all have potential hazards associated with them. Many local recreational pitches may have litter that is dangerous to sports participants. Large stones, broken glass and discarded hypodermic needles can cause serious injury.

Weather conditions

The weather can cause problems for the athlete. For example, in a thunderstorm there is a risk of being struck by lightening especially in water-based activities. Severe hot weather can cause dehydration and heat exhaustion, and severe cold weather can cause hypothermia.

Inappropriate or dangerous clothing

When you participate in sport, whatever your level of ability – this may be a 'kick around' in the park or preparing for an Olympic final – you must wear the correct clothing for the activity. Certain items of clothing can be dangerous if they get in the way of safe activity, for example training shoes must be laced correctly to avoid them coming off. Jewellery should not be worn if you are participating in activities where it may injure others, for example a necklace getting caught in the clothing of an opponent and causing a serious cut to the neck. Clothing should also be appropriate to the weather conditions. If the weather is very hot then obviously you will wear lighter clothes, and if it is very cold then it is important to wear enough clothes to keep warm.

Definition

Hypothermia

Hypothermia involves a drop in the body's core temperature. If the core temperature drops to 35 degrees Celsius or below then the person is deemed to be suffering from hypothermia. If the core temperature continues to drop then there is a real risk of death.

Lifting and carrying equipment

There are many instances of back strains and even broken limbs caused by lifting and carrying sports equipment incorrectly. For example, if carried incorrectly heavy gymnastic equipment is a hazard to the health and safety of the carrier and also to others who may be around at the time. Correct techniques should be employed when lifting equipment, and those working in sports centres are taught to bend their legs rather than their backs to lift, thereby protecting the back from injury. Putting up a trampoline, for example, should only be done by trained individuals because there is a danger that the trampoline's legs may spring up and cause injury.

Inappropriate or damaged equipment

The equipment that is used in sport should also be correct for the activity and the age/ability of the sportspeople involved. For example, in gymnastics the vaulting box should be at an appropriate height; for very young novice tennis players the rackets may be lighter and smaller than full size. If the equipment is inappropriate then injury may occur. For example, if a vaulting box is too high then there is a greater chance of the gymnast colliding with it. A tennis player who has a racket that is too heavy may well suffer muscle strains in the arm. Damaged equipment can also cause injury. For example, a damaged basketball backboard may well become loose and fall on a competitor causing serious injury.

Behaviour of other participants

It is important to behave correctly in sport to prevent injury. If a child throws a discus out of turn then this may well hit another child and cause a nasty injury. If a team player becomes overly aggressive and hits out at an opponent then again injury may occur. In outdoor activities, if a participant in canoeing decides to tip someone else out of their canoe then there is a risk of serious injury or even drowning. It is important to establish codes of behaviour so that all participants know what is expected of them when playing a particular sport.

2.2 Minimising and preventing sports injuries

The following are ways of helping to prevent the injuries or health problems identified above.

Physical fitness

Make sure that you are fit for sport. If you are to participate in an activity requiring stamina, make sure that you have good cardio-respiratory fitness (more on this in Chapter 3). For example, in basketball, make sure that you have worked on your flexibility in

Figure 2.4 There may be a risk of serious injury or even drowning

order to prevent injury if you are required to stretch suddenly. Be aware of the main principles of fitness training (these are covered in Chapters 3 and 6). Any training programme must take into account the individual. The sportsperson's age, the time and equipment available and the skill level must all be considered before the principles of training are applied.

Skill/technique

Each player must get to a particular skill level and have good technique before they can perform effectively in sport. Training should include basic skills that, when practised enough, become almost second nature. Injury becomes less likely as your personal skill level improves. Ensure that skills and techniques follow technical models of how the skill ought to be performed to ensure personal health and safety.

Preparation

Whatever the level of the sport or whether it is serious competition or just recreational play, you should prepare for the activity by carrying out an effective warm-up. This often includes some light activity to raise the body's temperature and to ensure better flexibility in muscles and ligaments. In team games the activity may include steady jogging followed by a series of stretching exercises to prepare the muscles for sudden and prolonged movement. A cool-down is equally important and should take place immediately after exercise. The cool-down normally involves similar exercises to the warm-up – steady jogging and stretching. This enables the dispersal of any lactic acid and prevents muscle soreness during the days following the activity.

In practice

Warming up for golf
Nick Dougherty
Golf professional
Upcoming golf star, Dougherty, recommends stretching your arms by raising them above your head, keeping your palms together. He then stretches the fingertips on the left hand higher than the right and then those on the right higher than the left. To loosen up he hits around fifty practice shots before beginning a round.
(Adapted from BBC Sport web site, 2004)

Training practice

Always ensure that your training is safe. After warming up sufficiently your exercise regime should suite your age, ability and physical fitness. You should also ensure that you do not push yourself too hard and that you listen to your body and stop if any exercise hurts or if you are getting unduly fatigued.

In practice

Training safely

The essential components of any training programme include the following:

- *Identify the individual's training goal.*
- *Identify the macro-, meso- and micro-cycles.*
- *Identify the fitness components to be improved.*
- *Establish the energy systems to be used.*
- *Identify the muscle groups that will be used.*
- *Evaluate the fitness components involved.*
- *Use a training diary.*
- *Vary the programme to maintain motivation.*
- *Include rest in the programme to enable recovery.*
- *Evaluate and reassess goals.*

The above aspects of training will be dealt with in detail in Chapter 3.

Coaches and performers often use specific goals associated with phases or periods of training and these periods of time can be split up into shorter-term goals. There are three recognised periods or units of time:

- **Macro-cycle** – this is the number of weeks making up the whole training period, e.g. 52 weeks.
- **Meso-cycle** – this is a set number of weeks to attain short-term goals, e.g. eight weeks.
- **Micro-cycle** – this is the short phase (usually one week) that is repeated up to the end of the meso-cycle.

Eating and drinking correctly

Participants in sport should have a balanced diet that ensures they have all of the required nutrients and enough water. Chapter 3 deals with diet in more detail.

For a healthy diet it is important to eat enough fruit and vegetables. This helps to reduce the likelihood of coronary heart disease and some cancers. There are government guidelines that suggest you should eat at least five portions of fruit and vegetables each day. Most healthy-eating guidelines warn against eating too much salt. If your diet contains too much salt then this may lead to high blood pressure which can cause heart and kidney disease. The athlete may lose up to one litre of water per hour during endurance exercise; therefore rehydration is essential especially in hot conditions.

The athlete needs to drink plenty of water during and after exercise even if they are not thirsty.

A sportsperson, whether a serious competitor or a casual participant, should not drink too much alcohol because this interferes with health and fitness levels. Fitness-enhancing drugs are of course banned and they should never be taken because of the many health risks. If caught taking them you are likely to be banned from competition and labelled as a cheat!

Safe equipment, clothing and environment

Make sure that all equipment is 'fit for purpose', in other words ensure it is in good working order and is safe to use. Clothing for sport should also be suitable for the activity; it should provide enough warmth and it should not be hazardous to the owner and others around them. Any playing surfaces should also be safe. For example, football pitches should be checked for broken glass or large stones and the basketball court should be dry and not slippery.

Correct lifting and carrying procedures

If you have to lift or carry sports equipment ensure that you follow the relevant guidelines. For example, get help to lift a heavy piece of equipment or use a machine/device that helps you to lift it. Instructions/guidelines must be followed closely, otherwise injury can occur.

III In practice
Examples of injuries in sport and leisure
Injury statistics (Health and Safety Executive)

The injuries in the report cover the five-year period from 1994/95 to 1998/99.

There were three fatal injuries occurring in the sports and recreation industry: one death involved being struck by a vehicle; another resulted from an explosion; and one resulted from coming into contact with moving machinery.

Fatal injuries to members of the public:

'A child was crushed by an unsecured mobile goal post while playing on a football field. Children moved the posts from their usual secured storage place so that they could use them. The goal posts were very heavy and unstable, and needed secure fixing before use.'

'A man died when his jet ski collided with a similar water craft piloted by a friend. The jet skis had been inspected and serviced by the proprietor of the jet ski centre. Observers said the two men were not observing sufficient caution while piloting the craft. The coroner reported a verdict of accidental death. No blame was attached to the proprietors. An engineer found the craft to be in perfect working order.'

'A member of the public was killed when he crashed at a motor racing circuit. The man had been taking part in a motorcycle "experience" activity. The rider died as a result of head injuries sustained in the accident. The investigation revealed that there was no obvious cause of the accident.'

Of the 999 major injuries:
- 349 (35%) injuries resulted from a slip or trip (106 involved slipping on a slippery surface; 75 involved lost footing; 62 involved falling over an obstruction; and 60 involved slipping whilst playing sports).
- 227 (23%) injuries resulted from a fall from a height (97 involved a fall from an animal, 30 involved a fall down stairs; and 25 resulted from a fall from another object).
- 95 (10%) injuries resulted from being struck by a moving or falling object (17 involved being struck by an object falling from a shelf, table or stack; 15 people were struck by a door or ramp; 11 involved being struck by a falling piece of structure; and 11 involved being struck by flying debris or nails).
- 79 (8%) injuries resulted from handling, lifting or carrying a load (of which 39 involved an awkward or sharp object and 24 involved a heavy object).
- 68 (7%) injuries were inflicted by animals.

Non-fatal injuries to members of the public:
In the five-year period to 1998/99 there were 3675 non-fatal injuries to members of the public in the sports and recreation industry.

Of these 3675 non-fatal injuries:
- 1430 (39%) injuries resulted from a slip or trip (762 involved slipping whilst playing sports; 228 involved slipping on a slippery surface; 148 involved lost footing; and 122 involved falling over an obstruction).
- 1347 (37%) injuries resulted from a fall from a height (640 involved falling from an animal; 297 involved falling whilst playing sport; and 126 involved a fall from a motor vehicle).
- 319 (9%) injuries resulted from striking a fixed object (216 involved walking into a fixed object, e.g. a wall; 43 involved walking into or striking another person; and 21 people stepped on a nail or other similar object).

2.3 Rules and regulations in sport

The rules and regulations have been designed to protect individuals in the workplace and also those who participate in sport. If the laws, regulations and guidelines are checked thoroughly and followed properly then accidents are less likely to happen and people's lives are not put at risk.

Health and Safety at Work Act (HSWA) 1974

This Act has led to big improvements in the quality of sports buildings and equipment. It has also led to better working conditions for staff.

The Act includes: 'Securing the health, safety and welfare of persons at work and for protecting others against risks to health or safety . . . controlling the keeping and use of dangerous substances . . . controlling emissions into the atmosphere'.

▌▌▌*In practice*

The HSWA 1974 has been called an 'enabling Act', in other words it allows for further regulation without full legislation via Parliament. For example, after the tragedy in Lyme Bay in 1993, when four canoeists died following an outing from an outdoor activity centre, a further Act came into force – Activity Centre (Young Persons' Safety) Act 1995.

European Directives (1992)

The European Community passed various laws that relate to health and safety.

Management of Health and Safety at Work Regulations (MHSW)

This concerns how employers and employees manage their facilities, and ensures that adequate health and safety procedures exist.

Personal Protective Equipment at Work Regulations (PPE)

This concerns the wearing of appropriate safety equipment such as goggles and ear defenders.

Manual Handling Operations (MHO)

This relates to finding ways to make manual handling of equipment less hazardous.

Health and Safety (Display Screen Equipment) Regulations (DSE)

It is now commonplace for workers to spend many hours each day in front of a computer display screen. These regulations are designed to protect such workers by ensuring adequate training, work breaks and a suitable environment.

Figure 2.5 Safety measures have been put in place to protect those who participate in sport

Control of Substances Hazardous to Health Regulations 1994 (COSHH)

A hazardous substance is one that is toxic, harmful and corrosive or an irritant. In the leisure and recreation industry there is widespread use of chemicals for cleaning, hygiene and disinfecting. In particular, swimming pools have chlorine and ozone to keep pool water clean. These regulations concern the storage and use of such harmful substances.

The regulations for employers include the following:

- have a code of practice for the control of hazardous substances
- have a trained risk assessor
- inform all staff of regulations and published guidance
- make sure that only those hazardous substances that are absolutely necessary are used
- train staff adequately in the use of personal protection and emergency procedures
- have a system of maintaining control of these substances, e.g. the length of time that they are to be stored
- monitor the handling of hazardous substances.

Health and Safety (First Aid) Regulations 1981

To conform to these regulations a procedure for treating injuries must be in place. The leisure and recreation industry involves supervising and participating in activities that have risks associated with them. At times some people may not follow the rules, they may themselves suffer from a diagnosed or undiagnosed existing medical condition, and there are many chance circumstances that may result in injury.

One of the most important elements of these regulations relates to efficient recording of incidents, including the circumstances and possible causes of accidents. These records are important if risk assessments are to be reviewed and future accidents prevented. In the present climate of increased litigation, it is also very important to keep records in case there are legal proceedings following an accident.

Certain accidents or outbreaks of disease have to be reported to the appropriate authority such as the local authority's Environmental Health Department. Under the regulations, serious incidents must be reported. The regulations in this case are the Reporting of Injuries, Diseases and Dangerous Occurrences Regulations 1995, also known as RIDDOR.

Children Act 1989

This had a huge impact on the sports industry, especially work with children under school age (known as 'play work'). The Act contributed significantly to a greater emphasis on care provision and child protection. The Children Act 1989 was aimed at children under the age of eight, but its interpretation has had an impact on the provision for all children of school age. There has been growing demand for trained and qualified play workers, for instance, because of the worker to child numbers ratios. The staff:child ratio for children under eight should be of 8:1. Records must be kept of accidents, attendance and the names of all employees and volunteers.

There is increased awareness of child abuse and in the sport and leisure industry there are many positions of trust associated with children. The Act protects not only the children but also employees who can be accused of abuse falsely or accidentally.

In practice

Children Act 1989
Examples of guidance:

- *Do not get into isolated situations with children.*
- *Physical contact must be minimal and involve only non-sensitive areas of the body e.g. the hands.*
- *Use physical restraint only in emergencies.*
- *Show appropriate role model behaviour, e.g. do not swear, smoke or drink alcohol.*

Safety at Sports Grounds Act 1975

This Act is concerned with large sports stadia that have at least 10 000 spectators. The owners and managers of such stadia are criminally liable if the Act is not implemented and so it is a strong and important legislative act. The Act requires that:

- A stadium can only be used after a safety certificate has been issued.
- This certificate is only for the activities applied for in the stadium.
- A stated number of spectators is allowed in the stadium.
- There is a record of attendance.
- There are records of maintenance to the stadium.

This is a very important Act. In crowds, people's behaviour can be erratic and if they panic there may well be crush injuries resulting in death. The number of very large sports stadia in the UK has grown since the beginning of the twentieth century and there was little control over the numbers admitted to each stadium and how spectators were controlled. Consequently there have been some dreadful disasters:

- 1924 Football Cup Final – injuries and loss of crowd control.
- Disasters at Bolton Wanderers (1946) and Ibrox stadium (1971) prompted a public inquiry.
- 1986 Bradford – fire and 56 deaths.
- 1989 Hillsborough – disaster involving 96 deaths.

These disasters prompted more legislation to be enacted.

2.4 Types of common sports injuries

Head injuries

A common head injury in sport involves being knocked unconscious and suffering from concussion. In contact sport concussion is possible, but it is most common in boxing, skiing, rugby and football. It is caused by a hard blow to the head. When there is a violent blow to the head the brain bounces against the rigid bone of the skull. The brain's stabilising connective tissue and blood vessels may tear and this stops the normal passage of messages in the brain. The result is a feeling of headache, nausea, dizziness, increase in pupil size, vomiting and confusion. If the player has suffered light concussion then they can return to play after about 15 minutes of rest following a medical check. If they are unconscious you should check that the airway is clear and call a trained first-aider. A hospital visit is advisable. It may take at least a week for a full recovery to be made after severe concussion. Post-concussion syndrome can occur weeks or months later if proper treatment is not given after the injury.

In practice
Concussion
Concussion is common in collision or contact sports, such as rugby, football, skiing or boxing.

The Welsh rugby player, Alix Popham, was knocked unconscious after making a tackle during a game against South Africa in 2004. Popham could have suffered serious injuries had it not been for his team-mate Ceri Sweeney, who prevented him from swallowing his own tongue. Like all professional rugby players, Popham was forced to take three weeks off, even after having been passed fit. Concussed players can suffer for several weeks after the injury.

(Adapted from the BBC Sports Academy web site, 2004)

Spinal injury

Any injury to the spine should be treated extremely seriously. There could be lasting damage to someone's health and their ability to operate normally let alone to play sport. Damage to the spinal cord may cause very painful conditions. A break in the cord high up in the spine usually causes death.

If there is a suspected injury to the spine then it is important to get expert help immediately and not to move the injured person. Moving a person who has a spinal injury could make matters much worse.

In practice

In sport spinal injuries can be caused by incidents such as a collapsed rugby scrum or falling off a horse in equine events.

In practice

Lower back stress fracture for a cricket bowler

A cricket bowler can be put out of action for as long as a year if they suffer from a stress fracture in the lower back.

The nature of bowling can place terrible strains on the spine, literally cracking a bone. Most commonly, bowlers with a faulty technique or those who have bowled too much may suffer from this injury. The stress fracture means an extended period of rehabilitation, which requires hard work from both the physiotherapist and the injured bowler.

It is comparatively rare to see bowlers with highly developed stomach muscles (or six-packs) as for some time this has been known to develop muscles that only strengthen the stomach and do not support the lower back. Working with the physiotherapist, the bowler needs to develop the deeper stomach muscles, which effectively hold the vertebrae in place. Gradually this strengthens the support given to the lower back.

After injury the bowler must be cautious and take reasonable steps not to aggravate the injury. They will take a day off after training and avoid indoor bowling practice, as the hard floor increases the impact on the joints. Warming up, and loosening the spine before exercise, remains essential.

(Adapted from BBC web site, 2004)

Fractures

Bone fractures can be serious injuries.

As well as damaging the bone, fractures often injure the tissues around the bone such as tendons, ligaments, muscles and the skin.

Anyone involved in contact sports is in danger of sustaining a fractured bone. For example, Martin Keown broke his leg before the World Cup in 2002.

A fracture occurs when there is a physical impact to the arm, leg or bone or an indirect blow.

There are different types of fracture:
- Transverse – straight across the bone.
- Oblique – diagonal break across the bone.
- Spiral – around the bone.
- Comminuted – bone is shattered.
- Compound fracture – this is also called an open fracture. This is a more serious fracture because the bone breaks through the surface of the skin. This fracture causes much more damage to the surrounding tissue and there can be serious bleeding. The exposed broken bone is also open to infection if not treated immediately.

When there is a fracture there is swelling and progressive bruising and a lot of pain during movement. You may also be able to see that the limb with the suspected fracture looks awkward and that the bone is not in the right place.

Cover and elevate the injured limb and keep it completely still. Go to hospital for treatment. The limb will probably be put in a cast to keep it completely still while the bone heals.

Casts can be made of plaster, which may be quite heavy, but doctors are increasingly using lightweight plastic casts. The injured player can be back in training after 5–12 weeks.

In practice

Fractures of the metatarsals

Striker Wayne Rooney was forced to limp off after 27 minutes in the Euro 2004 quarter-final against Portugal. He had to watch England be knocked out of the competition after his collision with the Portuguese player, Jorge Andrade.

Rooney had suffered the same fate as both David Beckham and Gary Neville; they had been stricken with metatarsal injuries just before the World Cup finals in 2002.

All three England players suffered a direct blow to the foot, or were affected by a stress fracture in the same area. Unfortunately metatarsal injuries are common in both football and other athletic sports.

(Adapted from BBC web site, 2004)

Metatarsals are the five long bones in the forefoot. These bones can be fractured as a result of impact (for example someone stamping on your foot) or through overuse (stress fractures).

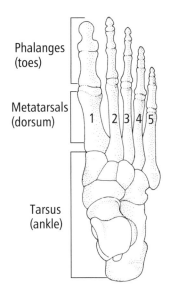

Phalanges
(toes)

Metatarsals
(dorsum)   1 2 3 4 5

Tarsus
(ankle)

Figure 2.6 Metatarsal injuries are common in athletes

The symptoms include pain in the bone during exercise and swelling and tenderness in the foot.

Treatment involves rest. An injured person may be asked to wear walking boots or stiff-soled shoes to protect the fracture while it heals. Recovery from a metatarsal fracture can take between four to six weeks.

Dislocations

This involves movement of a joint from its normal location and is caused by a blow or a fall. When a joint has a lot of pressure put on it in a certain direction, the bones that join within the joint disconnect. The joint capsule and ligaments often tear because of the movement of the bones. A dislocated joint looks unusual, out of place and misshapen. The sports person will have limited movement and will experience severe pain.

Soft-tissue injuries

These are injuries that affect muscles, tendons, ligaments and the skin.

Sprain

This is a tear to a ligament and is often caused by an overstretch. Ankles, knees and wrists are very susceptible to sprains.

▌▌ *In practice*

The ankle sprain

This is common for anyone involved in sport or outdoor activities. Going over on your ankle causes the sprain; sometimes a 'snap' or 'tear' is felt or heard.

There are three grades of severity:

- *grade 1: pain turning foot in or out*
- *grade 2: pain and swelling*
- *grade 3: huge swelling and problems walking.*

The following are required to treat an ankle sprain: rest, ice, compression and elevation. Do not remove the shoe until ice has reduced the ankle swelling.

Recovery takes between one week and three months depending on the grade of injury. The usual recovery time is two weeks.

Strain

This is a twist or tear to a muscle or a tendon. It is caused by overusing the joint, force or overstretching. There are three degrees of strain:

1   First degree – this is when only a few muscle fibres are torn and there is mild swelling. There is only a little pain.
2   Second degree – this is when there is a little more tearing of the muscle fibres. There is much more pain and there is swelling and stiffness.

3   Third degree – this is when there is a total rupture or tear in the muscle. There is a considerable amount of pain and there is severe swelling.

Others

Blisters

These can be a real nuisance to sports performers. A blister is the body's way of trying to put protection between the skin and what is causing friction, for example, in a footballer's case, their boot.

The skin has various layers. Friction and force cause these layers to tear. Fluid called serum flows in between the damaged skin layers producing a bubble of liquid. The pain comes about when this swelling rubs against another surface.

In practice

Blisters in Portugal Euro 2004

Blisters forced David Beckham, Sol Campbell and Steven Gerrard to miss training ahead of England's Euro 2004 game against Switzerland.

This could have been due to the very hot weather – heat causes the foot to swell. This can be made worse if the players have been wearing sandals or walking around in bare feet. If this is the case, then their boots may not fit comfortably.

Footballers put their feet through an enormous amount of stress. For example, when they jump for a header, the body's entire weight comes down on a very small area. That's a huge amount of pressure.

To treat blisters, the first thing you have to do is cleanse the skin with a sterilising solution. Then puncture the blister with a sterilised needle. Make sure you do not damage the skin any more, or it could create further problems. The next step is to put a protective covering over the blister to prevent infections. Chiropodists use something called hydrogel; it is like a second skin and protects the foot from further damage.

The healing time depends upon the size of the blister, but on average it is a couple of days.

The most important thing to remember is to put a protective barrier around a blister until it heals. Blood blisters are a mix of blood and serum. Some can be up to three or four inches in width and length.

Footballers can prevent blisters by wearing-in their football boots properly to soften up the leather. Wearing them around the house will help to mould the boot to the foot's shape.

Figure 2.7 Tennis players often suffer from tennis elbow

Tennis elbow

This is a very painful injury that occurs to the outside of the elbow where the tendons that bend the wrist become inflamed. These tendons attach to the bony part of the outer elbow bone called the lateral epicondyle. The scientific name for the injury is lateral epicondylitis, meaning inflammation to the outside elbow bone. We refer to it as tennis elbow as tennis players often suffer from it.

It is caused by the repetitive nature of hitting thousands and thousands of tennis balls. Tiny tears develop in the forearm tendon attachment at the elbow. The pain starts slowly but increases to a point where hitting the ball, especially a backhand shot, becomes virtually impossible. If you rest your arm as soon as the discomfort appears, then these micro-tears will heal. However, if you keep on playing, the micro-tears will become bigger, eventually causing pain and swelling that prevents you from hitting a ball properly.

Pain can stretch down the forearm to the hand, and it is painful to do simple things like holding a cup of tea or carrying a bag.

Treatment entails rest in order for the micro-tears to heal. The main cause of the injury is playing too much tennis, and complete abstinence is required. Other causes may be equipment related, such as too large a handle or a racket that is strung too tightly.

The best treatment for tennis elbow is a combination of:
- ice to reduce swelling
- anti-inflammatory tablets from your doctor
- soft-tissue massage to the tight forearm muscles and the injured tendons once the pain has subsided
- stretching the forearm muscles to help blood flow, and tissue-healing ultrasound therapy
- strengthening exercises for the forearm muscles and tendons.

Sometimes top tennis stars require cortisone injections or an operation if the injury does not respond to rest and physiotherapy.

Strengthening the forearm muscles that grip the racket and stiffen the wrist during backhand shots should help to prevent the injury from happening again. The forearm muscles and tendons should be stretched when warming up. An elbow brace may take the pressure off the injured tendon.

Technique adjustments may also help, for example playing the backhand shot more from the shoulders and less from the wrist. Reducing the amount of straight-arm shots by bending the arm at the elbow should help too. This will bring the shoulder and arm muscles more into play and take the pressure off the wrist and forearm muscles and tendons.

2.5 Situation assessment

When someone is injured in a sports activity, it is important to establish what is wrong with them. Any knowledge of first aid will be helpful, but it is best to get a recognised first-aid qualification.

Prioritise your actions. In other words, what should you do first and what should you do next?

You should:

1 Assess the situation. What risks are there to you and the injured person and to others nearby?
2 Ensure that the area is safe. Make sure play has stopped or other activities close by have moved away or have ceased. If someone has been electrocuted then turn off the electricity supply.
3 Give first aid – if you know what you are doing! Identify whether the person is conscious and then check the ABC (this will be covered in more detail on a recognised first-aid course):
A – Airway should be open
B – Breathing – check that they are breathing
C – Circulation – check their pulse.
4 Get help from a qualified first-aider.
5 Call an ambulance if necessary:
  - Dial 999
  - Ask for the ambulance service
  - Make sure you give an accurate location
  - Give clear, straightforward details about what has happened
  - Give some simple details about the injured person themselves, e.g. gender, age.

2.6 Alternative treatments

The medical profession is increasingly aware of and more tolerant of alternative treatments for injured sportspeople. There is no reason why alternative treatments should not be tried as long as the practitioner is appropriately qualified. Personal recommendation is best. If you hear of someone who has benefited from a particular treatment, get the details of the therapist.

Acupuncture

Acupuncture is a traditional form of Chinese medicine which has been in existence for over 3000 years. It involves inserting very fine needles into the skin at strategic places called acupuncture points, situated along energy channels called meridians. The Chinese believe that energy flows around the body in these channels. If it flows freely, the body is healthy but if there is a problem, energy stagnates and pain and other symptoms may develop. The

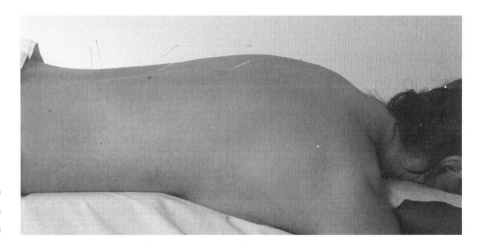

Figure 2.8 If energy flows freely, the body will remain healthy

stimulation of these acupuncture points clears the blockage and allows the body to return to a healthy state.

Yoga

Yoga was developed in India. It is a system of personal development involving body, mind and spirit that dates back more than 5000 years. The aim of this integrated approach of mind and body control is ultimate physical health and happiness together with mental peace and tranquillity.

Today yoga is practised for general health and for its preventive and curative effects.

There are various types of yoga, all of them leading ultimately to the same goal – unification with the Divine. The yoga paths can be broadly classified into:

* Bhakti yoga – path of devotion.
* Karma yoga – path of selfless action.
* Jnana yoga – path of transcendental knowledge.
* Asthanga yoga – path of Patanjali (eight-step path).

In the Western world yoga is recognised mainly as Hatha yoga which is a combination of asanas (physical exercises and postures), pranayama (breathing techniques) and meditation. Hatha yoga is in fact a single step in the eight-step path of Asthanga yoga. It is said to provide a balanced and wholesome approach to achieving perfect physical and mental health, happiness and tranquillity.

Eastern yogis believe that asanas are simply a stepping stone to higher paths and that working only on the body is a waste of time as the body is mortal whereas the soul is immortal.

Many people learn yoga by attending classes. However, videos and books teaching yoga are also popular. As with all exercises, technique is very important and for this reason it is advisable for beginners to seek out a reputable teacher.

Yoga can be practised by anyone at any age. It develops flexibility and muscular endurance and, like many of the martial arts, incorporates techniques to relieve stress and bring the mind and body into harmony. Yoga is the Sanskrit word for 'union' and means an experience of oneness or union with your inner being (self).

Figure 2.9 Yoga is good for general fitness as well as helping with injuries in sport

Homeopathy

Homeopathy is the treatment of like with like. Minute doses of substances that can cause signs of illness in a healthy person are used to treat the same symptoms in a sick person. Tiny doses of plant, animal or mineral materials are soaked in alcohol and then diluted and shaken vigorously. The more a substance is diluted, the stronger its therapeutic or helpful effect. Testing the substance on healthy volunteers and noting the symptoms produced determines the effect of each remedy.

Chiropractic

The most common forms of manipulation practised in complementary medicine are osteopathy and chiropractic. Physiotherapists also use manipulation techniques. Chiropractic focuses on the links between the spine and the nervous system. Corrections of spinal imbalance are believed to help restore the nervous system and improve internal organ function. Chiropractors generally use direct manipulation or quite vigorous massage techniques. Osteopaths also use direct techniques but often favour gentle manipulations, soft-tissue massage and subtle cranial (head massage) techniques as well. Manipulation has been shown to be beneficial for joint and back problems, especially low-back pain, neck stiffness and pain, and knee problems. It can also help relieve headaches and ear, nose and throat problems that are caused by restriction of the spine and muscle tension. Manipulation is the use of various manual techniques to rebalance the spine and joints of the body, to increase the range of movement of the joints and to stretch and relax the muscles.

2.7 Risk assessment

In order to prepare a risk assessment it is important to identify:
- The health and safety hazards in a given situation. This includes identifying equipment faults, use of chemicals, other substances hazardous to health and the possibility of spillages.
- The level of risk. The assessment is designed mostly to minimise injury to participants and workers. It is also designed to ensure that the activity involved can succeed without injury or accident but hopefully retaining the excitement and thrill of a sports activity. A safe environment is crucial if the activity is to be successful.
- The risks that are involved. Participants, coaches, supervisors etc. must be aware of their responsibilities in limiting the risks in any sports activity. The risks should be calculated, specialist equipment used and record sheets and other documents kept up to date.
- Procedures for monitoring or checking that risks are kept to a minimum. If there are any changes when planning an activity, these should be reviewed to identify their levels of success. It may be necessary to buy other equipment to make the environment safe, or new procedures may be required. All of this must be planned within an identified time cycle.

Figure 2.10 There may be obvious risks associated with the activity

Identifying hazards

The area in which the activity takes place must be checked carefully for hazards. The facilities and equipment used in sports activities often carry warnings of possible injuries and these must be taken into account.

In practice

An astro-turf all-weather surface can cause friction burns if a player falls or slides on the surface.

There may be obvious risks associated with the activity, the equipment or the facilities provided, for example in a swimming pool or in an athletics session related to throwing.

There are many risks associated with sports activities and without those the sport would lose its popularity as an exciting activity. However, with sufficient care and attention to detail the risks can be minimised. The main causes of accidents are:

- objects falling, e.g. a container falling off a shelf in a leisure centre
- trips and falls – a path leading up to a sports facility may be uneven
- electric shock – a faulty music system used for an aerobics session
- crowds – supporters at a football match, e.g. crush injuries may occur
- poisoning – toxic chemicals used in a swimming pool
- being hit by something, e.g. javelin
- fire, e.g. in the changing rooms of a sports centre
- explosion, e.g. in the store area of a leisure centre
- asphyxiation – caused by chemicals used for cleaning.

Identify who might be harmed

It is important to identify those who may not be fully aware of obvious risks, for instance children or those with learning difficulties, a person new to a job in a leisure centre, or a beginner in a sports activity. Once those individuals are identified, there should be an assessment of how they might be harmed. Safety procedures should be put in place to make sure that those involved are protected from harm.

Evaluate whether existing safety measures are adequate

There must be an assessment to show whether the risks associated with a hazard are high, moderate or low. If the hazard is particularly dangerous and the risks are high, then clearly more care is required.

Definition

Hazard

Something that has the potential to cause harm.

Risk

The chance that someone will be harmed by the hazard.

Figure 2.11 The risks arising from some hazards can be limited by using protective equipment

In many cases it may be possible to remove the hazard altogether, for instance an uneven path is put out of bounds or a broken indoor football goal is removed from the sports hall.

In some cases the hazard may have to be made safer in order to reduce the risks. For example, glass in a frequently-used door can be replaced with non-breakable plastic; a trampoline has additional safety mats placed around it.

The risks arising from some hazards can be limited by using protective equipment, for example cleaners wearing protective gloves or a rugby player wearing a gum-shield.

In practice

An example of a piece of protective equipment in sport is a pair of goggles worn by a squash player to minimise the risk of impact with the ball.

The hazard is often supervised so that the risks are minimised, for example a lifeguard at a swimming pool, spotters around a trampoline, or a coach supporting a gymnast on the beam.

Make a record of your judgements

Organisations that have five or more employees are legally required to record risk assessment.

Monitor, evaluate and revise the risk assessment regularly

It is important that assessments are reviewed regularly so that they are not out of date. After any incident that may have caused or nearly caused injury, procedures should be reviewed. If any aspect of the risk assessment was not accurate or realistic, then there should be a reassessment and procedures must be reviewed and changed if necessary.

Risk assessment pro forma

In practice

Operator ....
Address ....
....
Tel ....
Date of assessment ....
Assessment review date ....
Signed ....
Date ....

Activity – Flat-water kayaking introductory session (May–August)
Location site: Safe practice lake

Hazard	Who might be harmed?	Is the risk adequately controlled?	What further action is necessary to control the risk?
Drowning (generic risk)	Staff Clients	Buoyancy aids (BAs) to be worn at all times on the water. BAs comply with national safety standards. BAs undergo flotation monitoring to standards laid out in BCU Guidelines. Kayaks are also monitored to this same BCU standard. Staff are BCU qualified for type of water. Ratio of 1:8	All clients given a pre-session briefing – action in the event of a capsize is explained here. BAs sized and fitted. Checks are made by staff.
Hypothermia (generic risk)	Staff Clients	All staff/clients to wear warm clothing as appropriate. Wetsuit long johns can be issued at the discretion of the instructor in charge of the session. All staff/clients are issued with a waterproof kayak cag. A head covering is always used.	Staff judgement calls to be upheld. Established cut offs for sessions, i.e. wind onshore force 3, offshore force 2 max. (Beaufort Scale). Green Bay is a 'sheltered' site (in BCU terms of reference) with generally good landing points

(Adapted from British Canoe Union Guidelines 2004)

Progress check

1 Name 10 of the main risks associated with sport.
2 Choose one of the above risks and give an example of a sports activity where this may occur.
3 List three ways of minimising the chance of an injury in sport.
4 What factors should be taken into account when planning a safe training programme for a sports activity of your choice?
5 Outline the Health and Safety at Work Act 1974.
6 Name two regulations that are included in the Control of Substances Hazardous to Health Regulations 1994.
7 Identify three guidance points that you would make to anyone working with children in sport.
8 Name a sports injury that you or a friend has had recently. Give details of the injury and how you would treat it immediately after the injury occurred.
9 What factors should you take into consideration when planning a risk assessment in sport?
10 Give examples of low, moderate and high hazards in sport.

Preparation for sport

This chapter covers the essential theories and practices found in Core Unit 3 regarding effective preparation for sports performance. You are expected to be able to investigate the fitness level and lifestyle of an individual and to be able to administer simple fitness tests. This chapter will give you all of the information necessary to complete the task. You will be able to discuss the effects of lifestyle on sports performance and identify the different methods of training. This chapter will also enable you to plan a physical fitness training programme and to identify the nutritional requirements of sports performers. You will learn about the fascinating psychological factors that affect sports performance such as personality and motivation.

Learning objectives

- To understand the components of fitness, fitness testing and the effects of lifestyle on sports performance.

- To be able to plan a fitness training programme having understood the principles of training and training methods.

- To recognise the nutritional requirements of sports people.

- To identify and understand some of the main psychological factors that affect sports training and performance.

3.1 Fitness level and lifestyle

Components of physical fitness

The term 'fitness' is often used very loosely and frequently relates to aerobic endurance or how far you can run without getting too breathless. Fitness is more complex than that. It involves many different components or parts. Depending on the type of sport you are involved with, you may be very fit in one area but not another. For example, strength and power are very important to the discus thrower but less important to the archer. However, all sports activities require a good general level of fitness for all components. For some team games, for example, each component of fitness is equally important, although this may vary depending on what position you play. The following are recognised as the main components of physical fitness:

- **Strength**. This is the ability of a muscle to exert force for a short period of time. The amount of force that can be exerted by a muscle depends on the size and number of muscles involved as well as the type of muscle fibres used and the co-ordination of the muscle involved.

Figure 3.1 Strength is the ability of a muscle to exert force for a short period of time

- **Speed**. This is the ability of the body to move quickly. The movements may involve the whole body or parts of the body, for example arm speed in cricket bowling.
- **Power**. This is often referred to as 'fast strength'. Power is a combination of strength and speed.
- **Muscular endurance**. This is the ability of the muscle or group of muscles to repeatedly contract or keep going without rest.
- **Aerobic endurance**. This is the ability to exercise continuously without getting tired. The level of aerobic endurance is determined by the body's capacity to transport oxygen and the efficient use of this oxygen by the muscles.
- **Flexibility**. This is the amount or range of movement around a joint. The structure of the joint together with the muscles, tendons and ligaments restrict movement.

Figure 3.2 Speed is important for a fast bowler

- **Body composition**. This relates to the way in which the body is made up. The percentage of muscle, fat, bone and internal organs are taken into consideration. There are two main components: body fat and lean body mass (the latter is body mass without the fat).
- **Other components**. These are also important in determining how fit you are for sport and include:
  - agility – how quickly you can change direction and still maintain control

Figure 3.3 Good reaction time is important in order for a sprinter to get a good start

- co-ordination – the ability to perform tasks in sport, for example running and then passing a ball in rugby
- balance – the ability to keep your body mass over a base of support, for example a gymnast performing a handstand on a balance beam
- reaction time – the time it takes someone to make a decision to move. For example, how quickly a sprinter reacts to the starting gun and drives off the blocks.

Fitness tests

Fitness testing is important in order to assess the present fitness level of a performer. It also serves as a basis to measure progress. For example, after testing, a training programme may be followed and then after a few weeks another fitness test will reveal how effective the training has been and whether the performer has increased his or her fitness level.

As we have discovered, physical fitness involves a number of different components, therefore fitness tests must be designed to test these specific components.

It is important that individuals view the tests as benchmarks for their own improvements and do not compare them with the results of others.

Strength tests

Dynamometers can be used to measure strength, for example the **handgrip dynamometer**, which measures the strength of the handgrip.

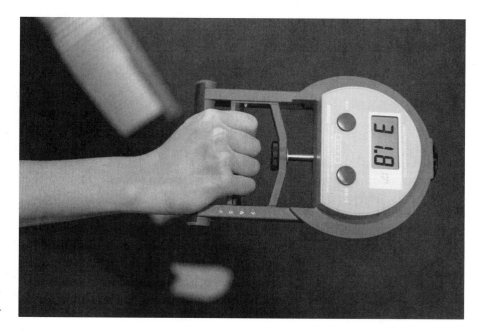

Figure 3.4 Handgrip dynamometer

Make sure that the handgrip is adjusted to fit the subject's hand. The subject should stand, holding the dynamometer parallel to the side of the body, with the dial facing away from the body. The handle should be squeezed as hard as possible without moving the arm. Three tests are recommended with one minute's rest between each test.

Speed

This can be measured by the **30 metres sprint test**. To prevent accidents this should take place on a flat, non-slip surface. The sprint should be a 'flying start'. The clock starts at the beginning of the 30 m stretch and stops at the end of it.

Cardiovascular endurance

The level of endurance fitness is indicated by an individual's **VO_2 max** – that is the maximum amount of oxygen an individual can take in and use in one minute.

▥ In practice

VO_2 max

Top endurance athletes such as marathon runners usually have a very high VO_2 max – approximately 70 ml/kg/min. The VO_2 of an average performer is about 35 ml/kg/min. A low VO_2 max of 25 or less would probably indicate that you are not going to be an endurance athlete. However, the more endurance training you do, the higher your VO_2 max scores will become.

The potential VO_2 max of an individual can be predicted via the **multistage fitness test** (sometimes called the 'bleep test'). This test involves a shuttle run that gets progressively more difficult.

The test is published in the form of a cassette tape by what was called the National Coaching Foundation (now known as Sports Coach UK). Subjects run a 20 m shuttle as many times as possible but ensure that they turn at the end of each run in time with the 'bleep' on the tape. The time lapse between each bleep on the tape gets progressively smaller and so the shuttle run has to be completed more quickly. The subject is deemed to have reached their optimum level when they cannot keep up with the bleeps. The level reached is recorded and used as a baseline for future tests or can be compared with national norms.

▥ In practice

The 'bleep test'

The test usually consists of 23 levels. Only the elite athletes can get into the top three levels. Cyclist Lance Armstrong and footballer David Beckham are two such examples.

The test is often recommended for players of sports that involve a lot of stop-start sprinting, such as tennis, rugby, football or hockey.

Muscular endurance

Testing the stamina of one particular muscle group can assess an individual's muscular endurance. One such test again comes from the National Coaching Foundation and is called the **abdominal conditioning test**. This tests the endurance of the abdominal muscle group by counting the number of sit-ups an individual can perform. The person does a sit-up each time there is a 'bleep' on the cassette tape. When the individual cannot complete any more sit-ups in time with the bleep, then it is deemed that they have reached their optimum level. This test can be used as a benchmark for training or for comparison with national norms.

Flexibility

This can be tested via the **sit and reach test**. The subject sits on the floor with their legs outstretched in a straight position. The subject reaches as far forward as possible whilst keeping the legs straight and in contact with the floor, feet pointing upwards. The distance from the ends of the fingers to the feet is measured. Using a sit-and-reach box as shown below ensures accurate measurements. Once again this test can provide measurements that can be used in assessing any future training and also for comparison with national norms.

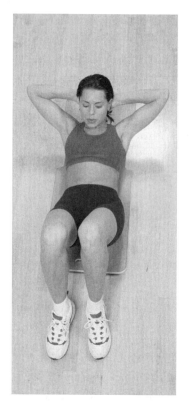

Figure 3.5 The abdominal conditioning test

*Figure 3.6
The sit and reach test*

Power

An individual's power can be measured using the **vertical jump test**. There are commercial jump test-boards that can be fixed to the wall. The subject jumps vertically, using both feet, and then touches the calibrated scale on the board with one hand. The location of the touch is noted. The test is completed three times and the maximum height attained is recorded.

Body composition

This can be assessed in a number of different ways:

- **Skinfold measurement of body fat**. This is completed using a skinfold calliper. Measurements of body fat are taken from the areas around the biceps, triceps, subscapular and supra-iliac. The measurements are added together and recorded to compare with national averages (called norms) or more importantly to assess training or weight management programmes.
- **Hydrostatic weighing**. Completed by measuring the water displacement when the subject is submerged in water.
- **Bioelectrical impedance**. A small electric current is passed through the body from the wrist to the ankle. Fat is known to restrict the flow of the electric current, therefore the greater the current needed to pass through the body, the greater the percentage of body fat.

The influence of lifestyle on physical fitness

Training for fitness is only one aspect of getting and keeping physically fit. Our lifestyle, that is, the way in which we conduct our everyday lives, can have a significant effect on our overall fitness for sport. The number of overweight people is increasing, as is obesity (the term used for extreme overweight). Many of us now live more sedentary lives, in other words we are less active. We use the car more for short trips rather than walking. There are more instances of diabetes and coronary heart disease, and these may be caused by the food we eat.

The main lifestyle factors that can affect our physical fitness are:

- **Stress levels**. Stress-related ailments are on the increase. This is often due to hectic lives that leave little room for relaxation. Modern life is very competitive, and for many the last thing they want to do is to get involved in competitive sport. However, others think that sport is a great release from everyday life and find participating in or watching sport refreshing and relaxing.
- **Alcohol, smoking and drugs**.

Alcohol consumption

Although alcohol is a concentrated source of energy, our working muscles cannot use this energy during exercise. Therefore many elite sportspeople do not drink alcohol and most drink very little.

Smoking

Few serious sportspeople smoke. There is overwhelming evidence that health and fitness is affected adversely by smoking, whatever age you are. Cigarettes contain tar, nicotine, carbon monoxide and other irritants that cause coughing for instance.

Normally haemoglobin in the blood carries oxygen. Haemoglobin absorbs carbon monoxide when it is present in the body, and once it has taken up carbon monoxide it is unable to take up oxygen. Therefore less oxygen is available for the body to work effectively. Up to 10% of the blood's oxygen-carrying capacity can be lost in this way.

In Practice

Smoking and sport

- *Time to complete exercise trials is increased after smoking.*
- *Endurance and capacity for exercise is reduced in proportion to the cigarettes smoked – the more you smoke the less fit you will be.*
- *Training has less effect on smokers – so you can train really hard, but smoking will undo all of the good work.*

Smoking is the biggest cause of preventable death in the western world. It kills more than 120 000 people in the UK every year, with most dying from three main diseases: cancer, chronic obstructive lung disease (bronchitis and emphysema) and coronary heart disease. Around 29% of men and 25% of women in Great Britain smoke. However, these figures are an average for the population as a whole – the figures for those on low incomes and from poor backgrounds are much higher. Half of all regular cigarette smokers will be killed by their habit.

Drugs

Drug taking involves the use of chemicals that alter the way we feel and how we see things, and it is one of the oldest activities known to man. The use of drugs, whether they are recreational (for example cannabis) or performance enhancing (for example anabolic steroids) is widespread and can seriously affect the health and well-being of a sportsperson.

Even when there are serious consequences to their use (as with tobacco, alcohol, cannabis, heroin or performance-enhancing drugs in sport), those consequences will not always deter a person from using their drug of choice. Due to the addictive nature of some drugs, it may be difficult to stop using them.

There is often more to an addiction than the physical withdrawal symptoms. Addiction includes anxiety, depression and the lowering of self-esteem. The pattern of these symptoms will depend not only on the drug used, but also on the psychological make-up of the person and the circumstances in which they are attempting to remain drug free.

UK Sport has been designated by the Government to deliver its policy objectives as the national anti-doping organisation, to represent the Government in international meetings and to co-ordinate the national anti-doping programme of testing and education and information for sport throughout the UK.

The core aim of the anti-doping policy in the UK is the planning and delivery of an effective programme that:

- protects athletes' rights to participate in drug-free sport
- actively encourages the support of medical professionals and administrators
- is publicly accountable for its plans and their outcomes.

A major landmark in the fight for drug-free sport was achieved in January 2002 when UK Sport published its Statement of Anti-Doping Policy. This was the result of widespread consultation both nationally and internationally and took over two years to develop. The policy set out the requirements of governing bodies and sports councils to deliver effective anti-doping systems. It brought the UK in line with all phases of the International Standard for Doping Control.

(Adapted from UK Sport web site)

In practice

Prohibited substances in sport

Prohibited substances may vary from sport to sport. It is the athlete's responsibility to know their sport's anti-doping regulations. In cases of uncertainty, it is important to check with the appropriate governing body or UK Sport and be sure to read carefully the anti-doping rules adopted by the relevant governing body and international sports federations.

(Adapted from UK Sport web site, 2004)

Athletes are advised to check all medications and substances with their doctor or governing body medical officer. When travelling abroad, all substances should be checked carefully as the ingredients of many products differ from those in the UK.

Certain substances and methods are prohibited in sport for various reasons including:

- performance-enhancing effects – which contravene the ethics of sport and undermine the principles of fair participation
- health and safety of the athlete – drug misuse may cause serious side effects which can compromise an athlete's health. Using substances to mask pain/injury could make an injury worse or cause permanent damage
- illegality – it is forbidden by law to possess or supply certain substances.

Most sporting federations have anti-doping regulations to ensure that all athletes compete free from drugs. The regulations aim to achieve drug-free sport through clearly stated policies, testing and sanctions. They are also intended to raise the awareness of drug misuse and to deter athletes from misusing prohibited drugs and methods.

Prohibited classes of substances
- stimulants
- narcotic analgesics
- anabolic agents
- anabolic androgenic steroids
- other anabolic agents
- diuretics
- peptide hormones, mimetics and analogues
- substances with anti-oestrogenic effects
- masking agents.

Prohibited methods
- enhancement of oxygen transfer
- blood doping
- the administration of products that enhance the uptake, transport and delivery of oxygen
- pharmacological, chemical and physical manipulation
- gene doping.

Classes of substances prohibited in certain circumstances
- alcohol
- cannabinoids
- local anaesthetics
- glucocorticosteroids
- beta blockers.

Other lifestyle factors

There are other lifestyle factors that affect your fitness levels. The amount of sleep you get can affect the way you feel as well as your sports performance. It is important to get enough sleep.

In Practice

The sleep habits of a top athlete

Haile Gebrselassie

The athlete keeps a regular routine, waking up at 6 a.m. and ensuring that he is in bed by 9.30 p.m. each day. With young daughters, he finds it difficult to sleep during the day and contents himself with a rest, usually lasting for about 2 hours in the afternoon.

Figure 3.7 The best athletes strive for a healthy lifestyle – that includes getting enough sleep!

Gebrselassie finds massage helps him, particularly in recovering from training and has a massage everyday during his heavy training periods.

(Adapted from BBC Sports Academy web site, 2004)

Physical fitness is also affected by the type of job you have. Some people have jobs that involve sitting at a desk all day – this is known as a sedentary type of work. Others who have active jobs may be more physically fit even before they train for sport. Diet also affects physical fitness and this is explored below.

3.2 Constructing a fitness training programme

To construct an effective training programme, it is important to understand the theory that training is based upon. Efficient training is based on what are called 'principles of training', that is, specificity, overload, progression, reversibility and variance.

Principles of training

Training programmes must take into account the needs and personality of the particular individual. The aims or goals of the training should be agreed. What are you trying to do? Do you want to prepare over a short or long period of time? The individual's goals must be understood, for example, does the performer want to get generally fit or fit for a particular sport? The individual's current

Figures 3.8a and b Before a training programme can be constructed, the needs of the individual must be taken into account

activity level must be assessed by doing an initial fitness test (see above). The person's age and skill level and the time and equipment available must all be taken into consideration before the following principles of training are applied.

Specificity

The training should be **specific** and therefore relevant to the appropriate requirements of the activity or the type of sport involved. For example, a marathon runner would carry out more aerobic or stamina training because the event is mostly aerobic in nature. It is not just energy systems that have to match the sport; muscle groups and actions involved in the event also have to be trained specifically. For example, a high-jumper would work on building power in the legs. However, there is a general consensus that good all-round fitness is required before any high degree of specificity can be attempted.

Overload

This principle states that you need to work the body harder than normal so that there is some stress and discomfort on the body's systems and parts. The body will become fitter and physical progress will follow overload because the body will respond by coping or **adapting to** the stress experienced. For example, in weight training

*Figures 3.9a and b
Training should be specific
and therefore relevant to the
appropriate needs of the
activity or the type of sport
involved*

*Figure 3.10 In weight
training the lifter
will eventually
attempt heavier weights
or an increase in
repetitions, thus
overloading the body*

the lifter will eventually attempt heavier weights or an increase in repetitions, thus overloading the body. The weightlifter will then adapt to this stress and be able to lift heavier weights.

Overload can be achieved by a combination of increasing the frequency (how many times), the intensity (how hard you train) and the duration (how long each session is) of the activity. These aspects are important if the **'FITT' programme** is to be followed.

Progression

The work done in training should become progressively more difficult so that advancements can be made. If the same level of exercise is attempted week in and week out, then the individual will achieve a certain level of fitness and will not progress from that level. Once adaptations or changes to the body's fitness have occurred then the performer should make even more demands on the body and do more strenuous work. You should not make too many demands of the body too early. Training must progress in a sensible and realistic way if it is to be effective, otherwise injury may occur and fitness levels will fall instead of progressing.

Reversibility

Fitness can deteriorate if training stops or decreases in intensity for any length of time. If training is stopped, then the fitness gained will be largely lost. For instance, VO_2 max and muscle strength may decrease. Therefore it is important to maintain your training. If you wish to improve your fitness significantly, it is better to have days of light training rather than no training at all.

Variance

There should be variety in training methods. A lot of different types of training or different activities will make training interesting and exciting. If training is too predictable, then performers may become demotivated and bored. Overuse injuries such as muscle strains (see Chapter 2) are also common when one muscle group or part of the body is trained too repeatedly. Variance in training can motivate and also help to prevent injury.

Warm-ups and cool-downs

See Chapter 2 for details on warm-ups and cool-downs.

3.3 Training methods

Aerobic and anaerobic fitness training

Aerobic capacity can be improved through continuous, steady-state (sub-maximal) training. The rhythmic exercise of aerobics or continuous swimming or jogging are good for aerobic fitness.

Definition

FITT

F = Frequency of training (number of training sessions each week)

I = Intensity of the exercise undertaken

T = Time that the training takes (duration)

T = Type of training that fulfils specific needs

Figure 3.11 Continuous swimming is good for aerobic fitness

This low-intensity exercise must take place over a long period of time, that is, from 20 minutes to two hours. The intensity of this exercise should be 60–80% of your maximum heart rate.

Anaerobic training involves high-intensity work that may be less frequent (for example a 100 m sprint), although elite athletes will often train both aerobically and anaerobically.

Interval training

This is one of the most popular types of training. It is adaptable depending on individual needs and sports. Interval training can improve both aerobic and anaerobic fitness. It is called interval training because there are intervals of work and intervals of rest. To train aerobically, there should be less-intensive and longer intervals. This is suitable for sports like athletics and swimming and for team games like hockey or football. To train anaerobically, there should be shorter more intense intervals of training.

The following factors have to be taken into account before the design of an interval training session:

- **Duration** of the work interval. The work interval should be between 3 and 10 seconds at high intensity for anaerobic training and 7–8 minutes for aerobic training.
- **Speed** (intensity) of the work interval. This should be 90–100% intensity for anaerobic and moderate (50–90% of work rate) if aerobic.
- Number of **repetitions**. This depends on the length of the work period, but up to 50 repetitions is appropriate for anaerobic. For aerobic, 3–4 is more appropriate.
- Number of **sets** of repetitions. Repetitions can be divided into sets, for example 50 repetitions could be divided into 10 sets of 5.

- Duration of the **rest interval**. This is the length of time that the heart rate falls to about 150 bpm. For effective aerobic training there should be a shorter rest interval.
- Type of activity during the rest interval. If the energy system is anaerobic, then perform light stretching. If aerobic then some light jogging may help to disperse lactic acid.

Fartlek training

This is also known as 'speedplay' training. It is good for aerobic fitness because it is an endurance activity and it is good for anaerobic fitness because of the speed activities over a short period of time. Throughout the exercise, the speed and intensity of the training is varied. An hour-long session, for instance, may involve walking (which is low intensity) through to very fast sprinting (which is high intensity). Cross-country running with sprint activities every now and again is a simple but reasonable way of describing fartlek training.

Figure 3.12
Fartlek training

Muscular strength, muscular endurance and power training

For strength and power training, the performer needs to work **against resistance**. The training is effective only if it is specific enough. In other words the training must be targeted depending on the type of strength that needs to be developed, for instance explosive strength for a thrower in athletics or strength endurance for a gymnast.

Figure 3.13 Training must be targeted depending on the type of strength that needs to be developed

Circuit training

This involves a series of exercises that are arranged in a particular sequence. It is called a **circuit** because the training involves moving around and working on a series of activities. Body weight is generally used in resistance training in circuits and each exercise in the circuit is designed to work on a particular muscle group. For effective training different muscle groups should be exercised, and the same muscle groups should not be worked consecutively. For instance, an activity that uses the main muscle groups in the arms should be followed, for example, by an exercise involving the muscle groups in the legs.

The types of exercise that are involved in circuit training include press-ups, star jumps, dips and squat thrusts.

Circuit training can also incorporate particular skills in the activities. For example, hockey players may include ball dribbling, flicking the ball, shuttle runs and shooting activities.

The duration and intensity depends on the type of activities that have been used. For example, a circuit might have one minute of activity followed by one minute of rest and the whole circuit could be repeated three times. Scoring is a good way to motivate people in training. It may be possible to time the circuit or add up the number of repetitions done in a certain time in order to give a score. Over the weeks it will be easy to see progression in fitness when more repetitions can be attempted or times are improved.

Weight and resistance training methods

In order for strength to be developed more resistance can be used in the form of weight training or using other types of resistance such as pulleys. Weight training involves a number of repetitions and sets according to the type of strength that needs to be developed. For throwing events in athletics, for example, training methods must involve very high resistance and low repetition. For strength endurance, for example in swimming or cycling, it is necessary to do more repetitions with less resistance or lighter weights.

Plyometrics

This type of training is designed to improve dynamic strength. Plyometrics improves the speed at which muscles shorten. If muscles have previously been stretched then they tend to generate more force when contracted. Any sport that involves sprinting, throwing or jumping will benefit from this type of training, as will players of many team sports like netball or rugby.

Plyometrics involve bounding, hopping and jumping. One type of jumping used in this training method is called in-depth jumping, which involves the athlete jumping on to and off raised platforms or boxes. This type of training is very strenuous on the muscles and

Figure 3.14 Sports involving sprinting, throwing or jumping will benefit from plyometrics

joints and a reasonable level of fitness must have been reached before it is attempted. As usual, it is important to stretch the muscle sufficiently before attempting this type of training. It is also important to have the right sort of footwear so that impact injuries do not occur.

Flexibility training

This is sometimes called mobility training. It involves **stretching** the muscles and this can help with performance and in order to avoid injury. There are two types of flexibility exercise.

Active stretching

This is when there are voluntary muscular contractions that are held by the performer for 30 seconds to one minute. The muscle is relaxed at the end of the stretching range. Muscle elongation may occur if this practice is repeated regularly. The stretching must be controlled and muscles should be suitably warmed up before starting to stretch.

One method of active stretching is called the **ballistic method**.

⫴ *In practice*

Ballistic stretching

The subject actively uses the momentum or movement of the limb to move the body through a wider range of movement. This is achieved through a bouncing-type movement and should only be attempted by those who are extremely flexible, such as gymnasts or certain athletes, because muscle tissue damage may easily occur as a result of such active stretching.

Passive stretching

This technique incorporates an external helper who pushes or pulls the limb to stretch the appropriate muscles. This is obviously potentially dangerous, so the subject must be thoroughly warmed up and should go through some active stretching initially. Gymnasts often favour this particular type of stretching. One type of passive stretching is called **proprioceptive neuromuscular facilitation (PNF)**.

⫴ *In practice*

PNF

This method of stretching involves trying to decrease the reflex shortening of the muscle when that muscle is stretched to its limit:

- *The limb is moved to its limit by the subject.*
- *The limb is then taken to its passive limit (that is, the limit of its movement without help from a third party) by the partner.*
- *Just before the point of real discomfort, the muscle is contracted isometrically for a few seconds, then relaxed.*
- *The muscle is then able to stretch a little more the next time.*

3.4 Nutritional requirements of the sports performer

Components of a healthy diet

Just like everyone else, sportspeople should follow a balanced diet that contains the right amount of nutrients necessary to live a fit and healthy life. The main nutrients are carbohydrates, fats, protein, water, vitamins and minerals.

Carbohydrates

These are made up of the chemical elements carbon, hydrogen and oxygen. Carbohydrates are primarily involved in energy production. There are two forms of carbohydrate:

- simple sugars – these provide a quick energy source and include glucose and fructose
- complex starches – these have many sugar units and release energy much more slowly.

Carbohydrates are very important to the athlete, especially when performing intense exercise. They are also essential to the nervous system and they determine fat metabolism.

Carbohydrates are stored in the muscles and the liver as glycogen, but in limited amounts that need to be replenished.
Sources of carbohydrates are:

- **Complex** – cereal, pasta, potatoes, bread, fruit.
- **Simple** – sugar, jam, confectionery, fruit juice.

When exercise takes place, glycogen is broken down into glucose which supplies energy to the muscles. When glycogen stores are depleted, there is less energy available and the athlete will become fatigued. It is recommended that carbohydrates should make up about 60% of a sportsperson's diet.

Fats

These are also very important and are a major source of energy, especially for athletes performing low-intensity endurance exercise. Fats or lipids are made up of carbon, hydrogen and oxygen but in different proportions to carbohydrates. There are two types:

- triglycerides, which are stored in the form of body fat
- fatty acids, which are used mainly as fuel for energy production. These are either **saturated** or **unsaturated**.

When muscle cells are readily supplied with oxygen, fat is the main fuel for energy production. This is because the body is trying to save the limited stores of glycogen for high-intensity exercise and therefore delay the onset of fatigue. The body cannot solely use fat for energy and so the muscle is fuelled by a combination of fat and glycogen.

Definition

Saturated and unsaturated fats

Saturated fats are solid forms, e.g. lard, and are primarily from animal sources. Unsaturated fats are liquid, e.g. vegetable oil, and come from plant sources.

Figure 3.15
Fat consumption should
be monitored carefully

III *In practice*

One explanation for marathon runners 'hitting the wall' is that the athlete's glycogen stores are completely depleted and the body attempts to metabolise fat, which is a slower way of producing energy, and therefore extreme fatigue is experienced and the muscles struggle to contract.

Definition

Amino acids

These are present in protein. There are eight amino acids that the body is unable to make for itself and these are called essential amino acids, for example leucine and threonine. The essential amino acids should be part of our dietary intake. The other 12 amino acids are called non-essential, for example glycine and glutamine.

Fat consumption should be monitored carefully and can cause obesity (see Chapter 4). Fat plays an important part in protecting vital organs and is crucial for cell production and the control of heat loss. It is generally accepted that a maximum of 30% of total calories consumed should be from fatty foods.

Examples of sources of fats are:

- **Saturated fats** – meat products, dairy products, cakes, confectionery.
- **Unsaturated fats** – oily fish, nuts, margarine, olive oil.

Protein

Proteins are chemical compounds that consist of amino acids, carbon, hydrogen, oxygen and nitrogen and some contain minerals such as zinc. Proteins are known as the building blocks for body tissue and are essential for repair. They are also necessary for the production of haemoglobin enzymes and hormones. Proteins are potential sources of energy but they are not used if fats and carbohydrates are in plentiful supply.

Protein should make up approximately 15% of total calorie intake. If protein is taken excessively then there are some health risks, for example kidney damage due to excreting so many unused amino acids.

Sources of protein include:

- meat, fish and poultry – the three primary complete proteins
- vegetables and grains – these are called incomplete proteins because they do not supply all the essential amino acids.

In practice

Protein breaks down more readily during and immediately after exercise. The amount of protein broken down depends upon the duration and intensity of exercise. Increased protein intake may be important during the early stages of training.

In practice

Calcium deficiency in sports people
Calcium deficiency may occur in females who are underweight, smokers, alcoholics, vegetarians and those who over-train.

Water

This is also a nutrient and is crucial for good health particularly for those who participate in sport. It carries nutrients in the body and helps with the removal of waste products. It is also very important in the regulation of body temperature. The body loses water through urine and sweat. This water loss accelerates depending on the environment and the duration and intensity of any exercise that is being undertaken. On average, individuals should consume about two litres of water each day. Those involved in exercise should drink more to ensure a good state of hydration.

Studies show that individuals who are dehydrated become intolerant to exercise and heat stress. The cardiovascular system becomes inefficient if there is dehydration and there is an inability to provide adequate blood flow to the skin – which may lead to heat exhaustion.

Fluids must be taken in during prolonged exercise. This will minimise dehydration and slow the rise in body temperature.

A number of sports drinks, containing electrolytes and carbohydrates, are available commercially. Some of the claims that are made about these drinks have been misrepresented. For instance, there are claims that certain drinks must be consumed to replace minerals lost due to exercise, but a single meal can replace these minerals perfectly adequately.

Water is the primary requirement during and after exercise because it empties from the stomach extremely quickly and reduces dehydration associated with sweating. Thirst is not a reliable indicator for fluid intake; therefore it is best to drink small amounts regularly even if you are not thirsty. In cooler conditions, a carbohydrate drink may give the extra energy needed in events lasting over an hour.

In practice

Dehydration in sport

The root cause of dehydration is loss of water, but more importantly the loss of blood salts, such as potassium. Loss of water and salt affects internal organs, including the heart, kidneys and brain.

The body attempts to keep a constant 37°C. Its most immediate reaction to heat is to trigger sweating. This leads to a loss of body fluids and in extreme circumstances dehydration can occur, as can heat stroke.

If someone is dehydrated the immediate symptoms are thirst, dry lips and mouth. In more serious dehydration cases the lips turn blue, the pulse is reduced and the individual is confused and breathing at a rapid pace.

It is imperative for athletes to remain hydrated. They do this in the following way:
- Take in fluids as early as possible on a competition day.
- Drink up to 600ml of fluid 2 hours before competing.
- Drink an additional 500ml 15 minutes before the competition.
- Bearing in mind that 15 minutes of exercise consumes up to 150ml of fluid, an athlete should replace this as soon as they can during the competition.
- Once the competition is over the athlete should drink as much fluid as possible to re-hydrate their body.

(Adapted from BBC Sports Academy web site)

Vitamins

Vitamins have no calories and are chemical compounds that are needed by the body in small quantities. They are an essential component of our diet because they are vital in the production of energy, prevention of disease and to maintain our metabolism. With the exception of vitamin D, the body cannot produce vitamins. Vitamins A, D, E and K are fat-soluble. Vitamins B and C are water-soluble.

A well-balanced diet will ensure sufficient vitamin intake. Vitamins can be found in fresh fruit and vegetables.

There is little evidence to suggest that supplementing the diet with vitamin pills can enhance performance and most excess vitamins are simply excreted in the urine.

Minerals

These also have no calories and are inorganic elements essential for our health. There are two types of mineral:

- macro minerals – needed in large amounts, e.g. calcium, potassium and sodium
- trace elements – needed in very small amounts, e.g. iron, zinc and manganese.

Many minerals are dissolved in the body as ions and these are called electrolytes. These are essential for the health of cells and the nervous system and for muscle contraction. Minerals can be lost through sweating and so there are implications for those who exercise. Minerals should be replaced quickly to ensure good health.

The following are examples of important minerals:

- Iron: This is an essential component of haemoglobin which carries oxygen in the blood. Iron-deficiency anaemia can impair performance in endurance events. Research has shown that 36–82% of female runners are anaemic and therefore should incorporate iron-rich foods in their diets. Only a qualified medical doctor should prescribe iron supplements because too much iron can be dangerous. Iron can be found in meat, fish, dairy produce and vegetables. The main sources are red meat and offal.
- Calcium: This mineral is essential for healthy bones and teeth. If there is a deficiency in calcium, then there is an increased likelihood of osteoporosis and bone fractures. For calcium to be absorbed, there needs to be sufficient vitamin D, which is produced by the body in the presence of sunlight. Calcium is found in milk and dairy products, green vegetables and nuts.

A healthy diet

The right balance in a diet is essential for health and fitness. Enjoyment is an important aspect of eating. A healthy diet does not mean that you have to give up all your favourite foods if these are considered 'bad' foods – it is the overall balance that counts. Balanced meals contain starchy foods with plenty of vegetables and fruit. The fat content should be kept to a minimum by using low-fat or lean ingredients.

Factors that also affect choice of foods include:

- culture; morals; ethics
- family influences

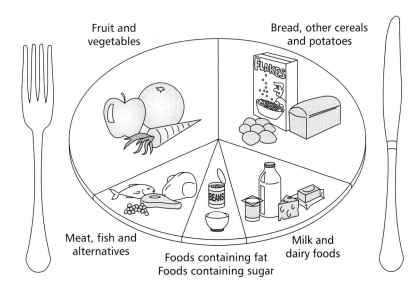

Fruit and vegetables

Bread, other cereals and potatoes

Meat, fish and alternatives

Foods containing fat
Foods containing sugar

Milk and dairy foods

Figure 3.16
A balanced diet
© *Crown copyright*

- peer-group influences
- lifestyle
- finance.

Eating sufficient fruit and vegetables is important for a healthy diet. It helps to reduce the likelihood of coronary heart disease and some cancers. There are government guidelines that suggest that you should eat at least **five portions of fruit and vegetables each day**.

In practice
What is a portion of fruit or vegetables?
- *2 tablespoons of vegetables*
- *1 dessert bowl full of salad*
- *1 apple/orange/banana*
- *2 plums*
- *1 cupful of grapes/cherries*
- *2 tablespoons of fresh fruit salad*
- *1 tablespoon dried fruit*
- *1 glass (approximately 175 ml) of fruit juice.*
                    (Adapted from Health Development Agency 2000)

Most healthy-eating guidelines warn against eating too much salt. If your diet contains too much salt then this may lead to high blood pressure which can cause heart and kidney disease.

In practice
Diet of a successful Olympic swimmer
Ian Thorpe, the Australian swimmer, restricts himself to a very precise diet. When he is at home he enjoys a breakfast of cereal, toast with jam and fresh orange juice.

Swimming is a sport in which the athlete expends huge amounts of energy; therefore Ian for the rest of the day restricts himself to low fat foods with a high carbohydrate component. He also ensures that he eats plenty of protein and fresh vegetables and tends to supplement fluids with isotonic drinks.

Ian will stick to this diet for at least six days out of seven. He manages to avoid pleasures such as chocolate, but admits that he is bored with his regular diet. One day a week he treats himself to a restaurant meal, allowing himself to eat whatever takes his fancy. He prefers Japanese food and in particular sashimi.

Ian admits that on his single day off a week he does indulge himself if he needs a snack. His preference is for Caramel Space Food Sticks, which are long, chewy and tasty energy sticks. Despite his dedication, Ian knows that he needs to eat normal foods sometimes in order to ward off the hunger pangs and by doing this one day a week he manages to stick to his diet for the other six.

(Adapted from the BBC web site, 2004)

Nutritional strategies in sport

Glycogen stores

Glycogen is crucial for optimum energy supply. One method of increasing the glycogen available in the body is by glycogen 'loading', sometimes known as 'carbo-loading'. This process involves the sportsperson depleting their stores of glycogen by cutting down on carbohydrates and keeping to a diet of protein and fat for three days. Light training follows, with a high-carbohydrate diet for three days

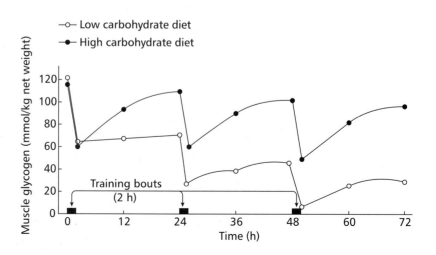

Figure 3.17 The influence of dietary carbohydrates on muscle glycogen stores

leading up to the event. This has been shown to significantly increase the stores of glycogen and helps to offset fatigue. When carbo-loading, the diet should consist mainly of foods like pasta, bread, rice and fruit. Generally a high-carbohydrate diet will ensure that glycogen is replenished during exercise.

Other energy-giving strategies include:

- consuming carbohydrates 2–4 hours before exercise
- consuming a small amount of carbohydrates within the first half hour of exercise to ensure refuelling of glycogen
- eating carbohydrates straight after exercise and for up to two days to replenish stores.

Fluids

The athlete may lose up to one litre of water per hour during endurance exercise. Therefore rehydration is essential especially in a hot environment. As we have discovered, thirst is not a good indicator of dehydration, therefore the athlete needs to drink plenty during and after exercise even if little thirst is experienced.

Sports drinks

Isotonic drinks

These are designed to quickly replace the fluids that are lost by sweating. They also provide a boost of carbohydrate.

Isotonic fluids are the most common drinks produced for athletes. They are particularly popular for middle- and long-distance runners.

The body prefers to use glucose as its source of energy. Sometimes it is better to consume isotonic drinks where the carbohydrate source is a concentrated form of glucose.

Hypertonic drinks

Hypertonic drinks are used to supplement your daily intake of carbohydrates. They contain even higher levels of carbohydrates than isotonic and hypotonic drinks (see below). The best time to drink them is after exercise as they help your body to replenish glycogen stores in muscles. These are your valuable energy stores.

In very long-distance events such as marathons, high levels of energy are required.

Hypertonic drinks can also be taken during exercise to meet the energy requirements. However, during exercise it is advisable to take them only alongside isotonic drinks to replace fluids.

Hypotonic drinks

Hypotonic drinks are designed to quickly replace fluids lost through sweating. Unlike isotonic and hypertonic drinks they are low in carbohydrates. They are very popular with athletes who need fluid without the boost of carbohydrate. Jockeys and gymnasts use them regularly.

The best time to drink them is after a hard workout. Hypotonic drinks can directly target the main cause of fatigue in sport – dehydration – by replacing water and energy fast.

Vitamin and mineral supplements

There is an increase in the body's requirements for vitamins and minerals if regular, intensive exercise takes place. This means that the athlete will eat more food because of the need for more energy. This in itself will mean that the body is receiving more vitamins and minerals. As we have already discovered, large quantities of extra vitamins and minerals can damage health, but supplementing the athlete's diet can be beneficial in certain circumstances.

⦚ *In practice*

Supplements

The use of nutritional supplements in sport is widespread.
Ergogenic aids *are substances that aim to enhance performance through effects on energy, alertness or body composition. Sports people are always trying to improve performance and give themselves a competitive edge that is not against the rules. Supplements can help but they could still be harmful in the short or long term.*

- *Energy: several nutritional ergogenic aids are effective at giving an increase in energy, for example carbohydrate supplements – whether in the form of powders, gels or sports drinks. During prolonged exercise, carbohydrates provide extra energy fuel to help prevent fatigue. Sports drinks deliver water and fuel to the body fast and so help in the avoidance of dehydration and fatigue.*

Several other ergogenic aids have been shown to be potentially beneficial for certain athletes. However, the long-term effects are still unclear – so unless you are competing at the top level, they are probably not worth the cost or the risk.

Creatine and bicarbonate supplements have been shown to be useful during high-intensity work. Creatine supplementation can increase muscle creatine phosphate levels for use in the adenosine triphosphate-phosphocreatine (ATP-PC) energy system. Alkaline salts, such as sodium bicarbonate (baking soda), can help to neutralise lactic acid and delay fatigue.

- *Stimulants: caffeine is performance enhancing as it stimulates the central nervous system. However, if you are competing, a caffeine level in the urine above 12 mg/l is not permitted. This level will be achieved by drinking about 500 mg caffeine (about seven cups of coffee) in a short time. Caffeine is also a diuretic, so make sure you keep hydrated.*

- *Body composition: a variety of supplements such as protein and amino acid supplements, carnitine, chromium and hydroxymethylbutyrate (HMB) claim to enhance performance by affecting body composition, either by increasing muscle mass and/or reducing body fat. But these have generally been shown to be ineffective.*

Factors to consider with sports performers and nutrition

There are certain aspects of the lifestyles of sports performers, especially at the top level, that should be considered when planning nutritional intake:

- timing of meals to fit around training and events
- ensuring that there is balance in the diet
- ensuring adequate fluid intake
- ensuring adequate iron intake
- diet should be suitable for very high workload, depending on the activity
- psychological well-being – if an athlete is unhappy with the diet, then even if it is physiologically beneficial, it could negatively affect performance because of psychological pressure
- sharing of ideas between coach/dietician and the performer to agree the best strategy depending on an individual's needs and perceptions
- obsession with food is common among high-performance athletes and should be avoided.

3.5 Psychological factors which affect performance

There is so much information about the way that the brain affects our performance in sport that there would be more than enough for many books! Core Unit 3 explores some of the main areas of psychology and sport including motivation, arousal and anxiety, personality factors and the way in which concentration and self-confidence can affect performance.

Motivation and sports performance

Being well motivated in sport is important, but some sportspeople seem to be better motivated than others. If you watch two athletes of very similar ability race against each other, invariably the better-motivated one will win.

Figure 3.18 Motivation

Some people do not appear to be interested in participating in sport, whilst others seem to be addicted to playing sport. If we could find out what motivates people to participate we could encourage more to be involved in sport and thus enrich their lives.

When we explore what is meant by the term 'motivation', most psychologists agree that it is to do with a driving force that encourages us towards behaving in a particular way. For example, an athlete may be driven to achieve a personal best in throwing the discus. The athlete is driven by the strong desire for self-fulfilment – to feel that they have challenged themselves and have won.

Intrinsic or internal motivation

Intrinsic motivation is the internal drive that people have to participate or to perform well in sport. Intrinsic motives include fun, enjoyment and the satisfaction that is experienced by achieving something. Some athletes describe the intrinsic 'flow' experienced during competition. They speak of high levels of concentration and a feeling that they are in total control.

In practice

A five-a-side football player who only plays occasionally and is 40 years old reports that when he plays he often feels a sense of relief from the day's stresses and strains and that he enjoys the hard physical work and excitement of playing football. This is a typical example of intrinsic motivation.

Extrinsic motivation

Extrinsic motivation involves influences external to the performer. For instance, the drive to do well in sport could come from the need to please others or to gain rewards like medals or badges or in some cases large amounts of money. Rewards that include badges or prize money are referred to as 'tangible rewards'. Rewards that involve getting first place in the league or getting praise from your parents are known as 'intangible rewards'.

Extrinsic motivation is very useful in encouraging better performance in sport. For instance, if a member of a gymnastic club wins a badge for reaching a particular standard, the badge is immediately recognisable as a sign of that person's standard, and that can motivate the individual to achieve even higher standards.

Arousal and anxiety

Over-anxiety to do well often causes high levels of stress. Motivation is important, but if personal drive becomes too great then

Definition

Extrinsic motivation

This is the drive that is caused by motives that are external or environmental. The motives are either tangible or intangible rewards.

Arousal

This is a term used for the intensity of the drive that is experienced when an athlete is trying to achieve a goal. High arousal can lead to high levels of stress, both physiologically and psychologically.

performance can suffer. 'Arousal' is another term for the amount of motivational drive that a sports performer has.

Hull (1943) suggested the **drive theory** to describe the effects of arousal on behaviour. This theory sees the relationship between arousal and performance as being linear:

$$\text{Performance} = \text{Arousal} \times \text{Skill level}$$

In other words, the higher the arousal, the better the performance. The more emotionally driven you are to achieve a goal, the more likely you are to succeed. According to Hull, behaviour that is learned is more likely to be repeated if the stakes are high. Figure 3.20 illustrates the drive theory.

Inverted U hypothesis

This theory has been applied to behaviour in sport. The theory states that as arousal increases so does performance, but only moderate arousal levels are reached. As arousal gets even higher, then performance starts to decline. Therefore, at very low levels and very high levels of arousal performance is poor, but the optimum level of arousal for the best possible performance is the moderate level. Figure 3.21 illustrates this theory.

In practice

A hockey player is well motivated and driven to win by her coach, but she keeps relatively calm and concentrates on the skills that she needs to perform. Her arousal level is moderate and therefore she will play at her best. This is an example of the Inverted U hypothesis.

Figure 3.19 High levels of stress are often caused by over-anxiety to do well

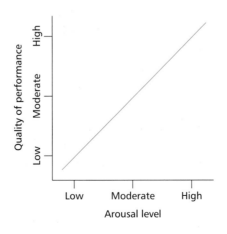

Figure 3.20 Drive theory

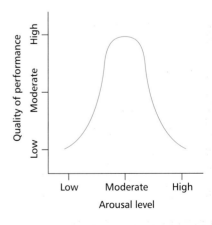

Figure 3.21 Inverted U hypothesis

Figure 3.22 A hockey player's arousal level is moderate and therefore she will play at her best

Research reveals that in sport the amount of necessary arousal depends on three factors:

- Types of skill – a higher level of arousal is required to perform a simple skill and a lower level of arousal is needed to perform a complex skill.
- Ability of the performer – the more expert the performer, the higher the level of arousal that is required to reach optimum performance.
- Personality of the performer – more extrovert performers need higher levels of arousal to perform well. If the performer is introverted then arousal levels are best kept low.

Anxiety

Anxiety involves worry that failure might occur and of course failure is always a possibility in sport because of its competitive nature. In sport, the desire to win sometimes becomes overwhelming. As Bill Shankly, the inspired manager of Liverpool Football Club, reportedly stated, 'Winning is not like life and death, it is more important than that'.

Some competitors can cope with anxiety and are mainly calm. There are others, including many top performers, who can become extremely anxious. There are two types of anxiety, described below.

Trait anxiety (a trait)

This is a personality trait that is enduring in the individual.

A performer with high trait anxiety has the predisposition or the potential to react to situations with apprehension.

State anxiety (a state)

This is anxiety in a particular situation.

There are two types of state anxiety:

- somatic – the body's response, e.g. tension, rapid pulse rate etc.
- cognitive – psychological worry about a situation.

Competitive anxiety is often experienced in sports competition. There are four major factors related to competitive anxiety:

- The interaction between the person and the situation. Some sports performers will be anxious in match situations but not in training.
- Anxiety can be caused by a response that is connected to a personality trait (called trait anxiety) or by a response to a specific situation (state anxiety).
- Anxiety levels may vary. Those with high trait anxiety are likely to become anxious in very stressful situations, but they are not equally anxious in all stressful situations.
- Competition factors. This is the interaction between personality factors, trait anxiety and the situation. This interaction will affect behaviour and may cause state anxiety.

Ways to control anxiety and arousal

The management of stress to eliminate anxiety and to control arousal is important, especially to high-level performers.

Stress management techniques are widely used by sportspeople to cope with high levels of anxiety. Increasingly sport has assumed huge importance not just for the performers themselves but for many other people too.

Cognitive anxiety management techniques are those that affect the mind and therefore psychological anxiety. **Somatic techniques** are those that affect the body directly, such as relaxation. Cognitive anxiety can affect somatic anxiety and vice versa. Controlling the heart rate using relaxation methods can make us feel more positive about performing. Positive thinking can, in turn, control our heart rate.

In practice

Jonny Wilkinson's strategies to keep calm

Newcastle Falcons and England

Like many professional sports people and athletes, this rugby professional ensures his state of mind is correct and that he has gone through his superstitious rituals before stepping out onto the pitch.

Wilkinson admits that he is both nervous and aggressive, psyching himself up for what he knows he must soon face. Wilkinson's own pre-match superstitions include wearing the same t-shirt under his England shirt. He never puts on his shoulder pads

Definition

Personality

The sum total of an individual's characteristics that make him unique. (Hollander, 1971)

Personality represents those characteristics of the person that account for consistent patterns of behaviour. (Pervin, 1993)

The more-or-less stable and enduring organisation of a person's character, temperament, intellect and physique which determines the unique adjustment to the environment. (Eysenck, 1960)

Personality is an overall pattern of psychological characteristics that makes each person a unique individual. (Gill 1986)

before he has warmed up. He does all of this subconsciously, making sure that he never puts on his England shirt before he has warmed up; feeling that as he has never done this, if he does something will go wrong. His rituals or routines help him control his nerves before a game.

In the dressing room Wilkinson's teammates also show anxiety and are always desperate to begin the game. They are sufficiently psyched up and, for many, even thinking about their state of mind before a match makes them nervous. Nerves are obviously a key feature and one of his unnamed teammates vomits into a bin before every game, due to nerves rather than superstition. Wilkinson admits, "people like to have their own routines to fight back the nerves to keep them sane."

(BBC Sport web site, 2004)

Personality and sports performance

Psychologists attempt to see links between certain types of people and success in sport. They also try to find links between types of personalities and the sports they choose to become involved in.

Personality profiles

Sports psychologists have put in a great deal of time and effort to build a picture of typical personalities of sports performers. They have attempted to show that there are major differences between successful sportspeople and those that are unsuccessful or avoid sport altogether.

Research has indicated that sports that involve physical contact, like wrestling, attract people with a different group of personality characteristics to those of the people that enjoy individual sports such as gymnasts. Team players have also been shown to be more anxious and extroverted, but they lack the sensitivity and imagination associated with individual sports performers. Links have also been established between player positions and certain personality characteristics. For instance, positions which require decision making, for example a midfield hockey player, need a personality that can concentrate, control anxiety and is confident.

Many psychologists group the personality characteristics into dimensions or scales: extroversion through to introversion; stable through to neurotic.

Each pair should be viewed on a scale or **continuum**. For instance, individuals may have extrovert and introvert traits, but they are slightly more extrovert than introvert.

There is another approach to classifying personality called the '**narrow band**' approach, and this states that personality characteristics can be grouped into two main types: Type A and Type B.

Personality characteristics

- **Extrovert** – seeks social situations and likes excitement. Lacks concentration.
- **Introvert** – does not seek social situations and likes peace and quiet. Good at concentrating.
- **Stable** – does not swing from one emotion to another.
- **Neurotic** – highly anxious and has unpredictable emotions.

- Type A – these individuals are impatient and lack tolerance towards others. They also have high levels of personal anxiety.
- Type B – these people are far more relaxed and are more tolerant towards others. They have much less personal anxiety.

Hinckle, Lyons and Burke (1989) researched the link between the narrow band approach and sports performance. Some 96 runners, aged between 16 and 66, were identified as either Type A or Type B personalities. There was no significant difference between the two groups, except Type A runners ran for longer when they were not motivated than Type B.

Different situations often trigger different personality characteristics. For instance, a netball player may only show signs of aggression when losing. Research has shown that there is a link between certain personality traits and the sports that are chosen for participation, but there is little evidence to support the view that knowing whether a performer is extrovert, introvert, Type A or Type B can predict performance.

Concentration and self-confidence

The ability to concentrate often depends on whether you are able to control the anxiety that you inevitably feel before or during sports competition. The amount of self-confidence that an individual has is very important in concentration and motivation.

Self-confidence can often be specific to a particular situation – Bandura (1977) called this **self-efficacy**. This specific confidence can vary from situation to situation and, according to Bandura, can affect performance if the individual is skilful enough. People who expect to be confident in a particular situation are more likely to choose that activity. People who expect to have low self-efficacy in a situation will avoid that particular activity.

Our thoughts about whether self-confidence is going to be high or low may determine the activity we choose, the amount of effort we put into it and whether we stick with the task or give up easily.

Factors affecting self-efficacy

Our expectations of self-efficacy depend on four types of information:

- Performance accomplishments. These probably have the strongest influence on self-confidence. If success has been experienced in the past, especially if it has been attributed to controllable factors, then feelings of self-confidence are likely to be high.

- Vicarious experiences. This refers to what we have observed before. If we watch others perform and they are successful, then we are more likely to experience high self-efficacy as long as the performers we are watching are of a similar standard to ourselves.
- Verbal persuasion. If we are encouraged to try a particular activity, our confidence in that situation may increase. The effectiveness of this encouragement depends on who is encouraging us and in what ways. Significant others are more likely than strangers to persuade us to have a go.
- Emotional arousal. Our perceptions of how aroused we are can affect our confidence in a particular situation. If you have effective strategies to control physiological and psychological arousal levels (perhaps the ability to relax or to use mental rehearsal) then you are more likely to have high self-efficacy.

In practice

Strategies that you could use to raise the level of self-efficacy of a high-jumper:

- *Try to give him initial success by lowering the bar to start with or using some flexi-rope.*
- *Demonstrate how it can be done or, if you are much better than him, use someone of similar ability. An actual demonstration (live modelling) can be more effective in raising self-confidence than a video recording.*
- *Verbally encourage the athlete. Tell him that he should 'have a go', that you think he will succeed – even that the mat is nice and soft!*
- *Tell him that to be worried is a natural, very positive response because it prepares the body well. Alternatively, teach him some relaxation techniques or how to mentally rehearse the activity (but be aware that this could increase his anxiety).*

Progress check

1 Name the main components of fitness.
2 Choose two components and describe how you would test the level of fitness for each.
3 Explain how lifestyle factors can affect physical fitness.
4 Give the five main principles of training.
5 What is meant by the interval training method?
6 What is plyometrics?
7 Why is the intake of water so crucial in sport?
8 What is meant by a healthy diet?
9 Give an example of intrinsic and extrinsic motivation – give sports examples for each.
10 Using examples from sport, explain the inverted U hypothesis.

4

The body in sport

This chapter covers the main scientific aspects of how the body responds before, during and after exercise. The theoretical aspects will be continuously related to sport in a practical and realistic way to prepare effectively for Unit 4: The Body in Sport. The main aspects of the skeletal and muscular structures and their functions in producing body movements during sports activity are described. This chapter also investigates muscle contraction, joint action and levers in relation to sports activity. There is a section on the structure and function of the cardiovascular and respiratory systems. This chapter gives a brief description of the short-term adaptations that take place during and after exercise as demanded by the unit criteria.

Learning objectives

- To enable understanding of the structure and function of the skeletal system and how it affects sports movements.
- To be able to identify the major muscles in the body and their role in producing movement for sport.
- To be able to describe the structure and function of the cardiovascular and the respiratory systems.
- To understand the short-term effects of exercise on the cardiovascular and respiratory systems.

4.1 The skeletal system

The skeleton has **four** major functions:
1 To give shape and support to the body – producing posture.
2 To allow movement of the body – by providing areas or sites for muscle attachment. This also provides for a system of levers (see below).
3 To give protection to the internal organs – such as the heart, lungs, spinal cord and brain.
4 To produce blood – red and white blood cells.

The **axial** skeleton is the main source of support and is the central part of the skeleton. It includes the cranium, the vertebral column, the rib cage (which includes 12 pairs of ribs) and the sternum.

The **appendicular** skeleton consists of the remaining bones and includes the girdles that join these bones to the axial skeleton.

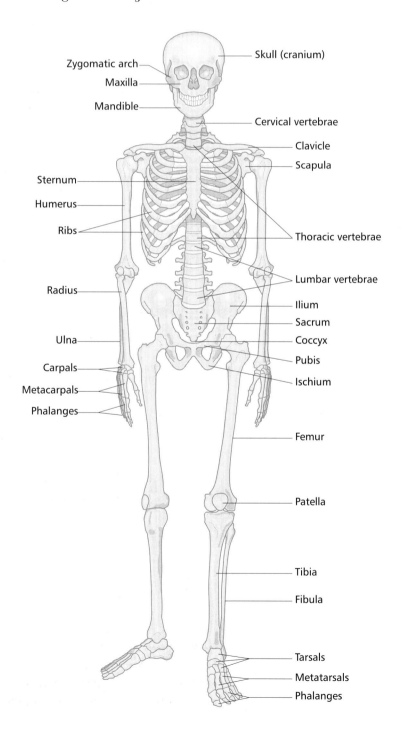

Figure 4.1 Major bones in the human skeleton

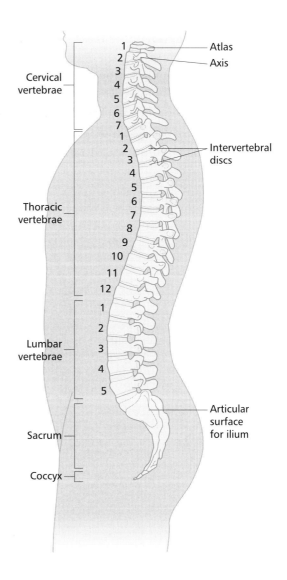

Figure 4.2 Lateral view of spinal column

Joints

There are many different types of joint in the human body including some that permit very little or no movement. Joints are very important in movements related to sport. There are three main types of joint.

Fibrous or fixed

These joints do not allow any movement. Tough, fibrous tissue lies between the ends of the bones, for example the sutures of the cranium.

Cartilaginous or slightly moveable

These joints allows some movement. The ends of the bones have tough fibrous cartilage which allows for shock absorption and also gives stability, for example the intervertebral discs in the spine.

Synovial or freely moveable

These are the most common joints and since they allow for a wide range of movement they are very important to sports participants. They consist of a joint capsule which is lined with a synovial membrane. Lubrication is provided for the joint in the form of synovial fluid. This is secreted into the joint by the synovial membrane, for example the knee joint.

Figure 4.3 Synovial joint

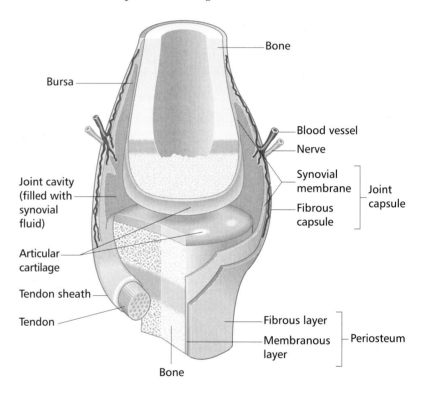

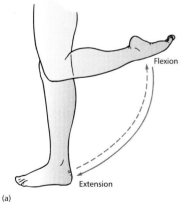

(a)

Figure 4.4 Movements possible at the knee joint: flexion and extension; inward and outward rotation (in a flexed, non-weight bearing position)

The following are types of synovial joint:

- **Hinge joint** – this allows movement in one plane only (uniaxial), e.g. knee joint.
- **Pivot joint** – this allows rotation only and is therefore also uniaxial, e.g. axis and atlas of the cervical vertebrae.
- **Ellipsoid joint** – this is biaxial, allowing movement in two planes, e.g. the radio-carpel joint of the wrist.
- **Gliding joint** – this is when two flat surfaces glide over one another and can permit movement in most directions, although mainly biaxial, e.g. the carpel bones in the wrist.
- **Saddle joint** – this is when a concave surface meets a convex surface and is biaxial, e.g. carpal-metacarpal joint of the thumb.
- **Ball and socket joint** – this allows a wide range of movement and occurs when a round head of bone fits into a cup-shaped depression, e.g. the shoulder joint.

Figure 4.5 The knee joint is used extensively in many team sports

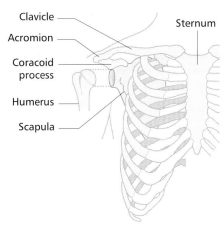

Figure 4.6 Anterior view of the shoulder girdle

Clavicle
Acromion
Coracoid process
Humerus
Scapula
Sternum

Cartilage

This is soft connective tissue. The skeletons of newly born babies consist of cartilage and as they get older this cartilage is mostly replaced by bone – a process known as ossification. Cartilage has no blood supply but receives nutrition though diffusion from the surrounding capillary network. There are three basic types of cartilage:

- Yellow elastic cartilage – this is flexible tissue, e.g. part of the ear lobe.
- Hyaline or blue articular cartilage – this is found on the articulating surfaces of bones, this protects and allows movement

Figure 4.7 The javelin thrower depends heavily on the shoulder joint

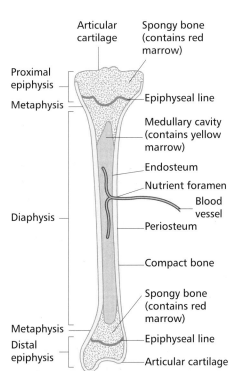

Articular cartilage
Spongy bone (contains red marrow)
Proximal epiphysis
Metaphysis
Epiphyseal line
Medullary cavity (contains yellow marrow)
Endosteum
Nutrient foramen
Blood vessel
Diaphysis
Periosteum
Compact bone
Spongy bone (contains red marrow)
Metaphysis
Epiphyseal line
Distal epiphysis
Articular cartilage

Figure 4.8 Structure of a typical long bone showing the position of articular cartilage

between bones with limited friction. Hyaline cartilage thickens as a result of exercise.

- White fibrocartilage – this consists of tough tissue that acts as a shock absorber. It is found in parts of the body where there is a great deal of stress, for example the semilunar cartilage in the knee joint.

Types of movement

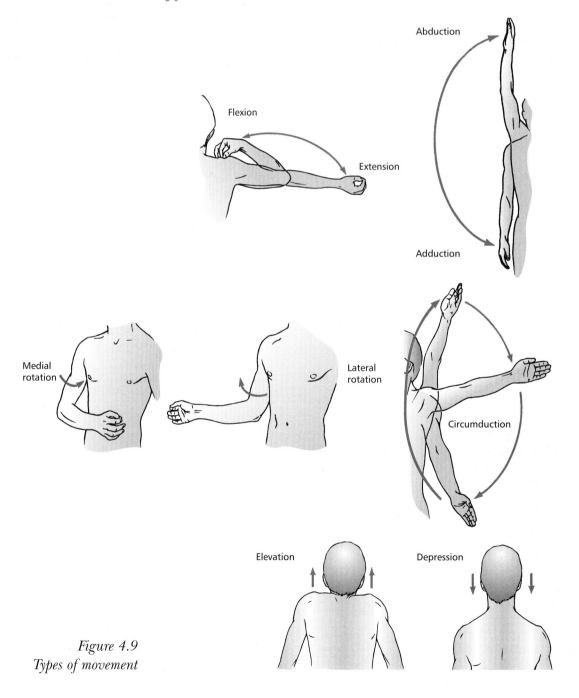

Figure 4.9
Types of movement

Figure 4.10

Figure 4.11

Flexion

This is a decrease in the angle around a joint, for example bending your arm at the elbow and touching your shoulder with your hand.

In practice

*In weight training the arm shows **flexion** at the elbow (see Figure 4.10).*

Extension

This is when the angle of the bones that are moving (articulating bones) is increased, for example from a stooped or squat position you then stand up. The angle between your femur and tibia (upper and lower leg) increases, thus extension has taken place.

In practice

*When a gymnast drives up from the floor to catch the bars, **extension** occurs at the knee joint (see Figure 4.11).*

Abduction

The movement of the body away from the middle or the midline of the body, for example lying on your left side and lifting your right leg straight up away from the midline.

In practice

*A gymnast with one leg lifted to the side of her body shows **abduction** (see Figure 4.12).*

Adduction

This is the opposite of abduction and is the movement towards the midline, for example lowering the lifted leg towards the middle of your body.

Figure 4.12

Figure 4.13

Figure 4.14

Figure 4.15

▌▌In practice

*In swimming the recovery of the legs from the breaststroke leg kick involves **adduction** (see Figure 4.13).*

Circumduction

This is when the lower end of a bone moves in the shape of a circle. This is really a combination of flexion, extension, abduction and adduction. The only true circumduction occurs at the shoulder and hips where there are ball and socket joints.

▌▌In practice

*A bowler in cricket moves the arm in a full circle thus showing **circumduction** at the shoulder joint (see Figure 4.14).*

Rotation

This is when the bone turns about its longitudinal axis within the joint. Rotation towards the body is called internal or **medial rotation**; rotation away from the body is called external or **lateral rotation**.

▌▌In practice

*A ballet dancer moves into first position and **rotates** the hip joint laterally (see Figure 4.15).*

Pronation

This occurs at the elbow joint and involves facing the palm of your hand downwards.

Figure 4.16

Figure 4.17

III *In practice*

*In table-tennis a player about to hit a ball with top spin shows **rotation** of the lower arm bones (see Figure 4.16).*

Supination

This is the opposite of pronation and therefore involves turning the palm of your hand to face upwards.

III *In practice*

*A discus thrower preparing to throw holds the discus and the lower arm is in a position showing **supination** (see Figure 4.17).*

Plantar flexion

This is at the ankle joint and occurs when you point your toes, with the foot bending downwards away from the tibia.

III *In practice*

*In a floor routine a gymnast may have pointed toes whilst balancing in a pose, or toes that are **plantar flexed** (see Figure 4.18).*

Dorsiflexion

This also occurs at the ankle when you bend the foot up towards your tibia.

III *In practice*

*When using the breaststroke leg kick during swimming the ankle shows **dorsiflexion** to enable the foot to push against the water and achieve more speed (see Figure 4.19).*

Figure 4.18

Figure 4.19

4.2 Major muscles

There are three types of muscle:

- **Involuntary muscle** – or smooth muscle, which is found in the body's internal organs. This is involuntary muscle because it is not under our conscious control.

- **Cardiac muscle** – this is only found in the heart and it is also involuntary.
- **Skeletal or voluntary muscle** – this is under our conscious control and is used primarily for movement.

The functions of specific muscles

The following muscles are named in the unit specification:

- Triceps – this is the elbow extensor (triceps brachii) and is attached to the elbow. Its function is to straighten the elbow and to swing the arm backwards, e.g. when performing a backhand in table tennis.
- Biceps – this is an elbow flexor (biceps brachii). Its function is to swing the upper arm forward and to turn the forearm so that the palm of the hand points upwards (supination), e.g. when performing a biceps curl in weight training.
- Deltoid – this is used in all movements of the arms. Its most important function is to lift the arm straight outwards and upwards (abduction), e.g. to make a block in volleyball with arms straight above the head.
- Pectorals – there are two sets of chest muscles: the pectoralis major (greater chest muscle) and pectoralis minor (lesser chest muscle). These help to adduct the arm and rotate it inwards as well as lowering the shoulder blades, e.g. a rugby player making a tackle would hold on to their opponent using the pectoral muscles.
- Trapezius – this adducts and rotates the shoulder blade outwards. It also helps to turn the head and bends the neck backwards, e.g. a rugby forward in a scrum will use the trapezius to hold onto opponents.
- Gluteals – these are the muscles in your buttocks. They straighten and adduct the hip, rotate the thigh outwards and help to straighten the knee, e.g. a sprinter will use the gluteals in the leg action of sprinting down the track.
- Quadriceps – this provides stability to the knee joint and extends or straightens the knee joint, e.g. a long-jumper when driving off the board will use the quadriceps to straighten the knee joint at take off.
- Hamstrings – these muscles will straighten the hip. They will also bend the knee and rotate it outwards, e.g. a netball player when running across the court will use her hamstrings to bend her knees.
- Gastrocnemius – or calf muscle. This is used to bend the knee and to straighten or plantarflex the ankle, e.g., a swimmer doing front crawl will use the gastrocnemius to point their toes during the leg action.

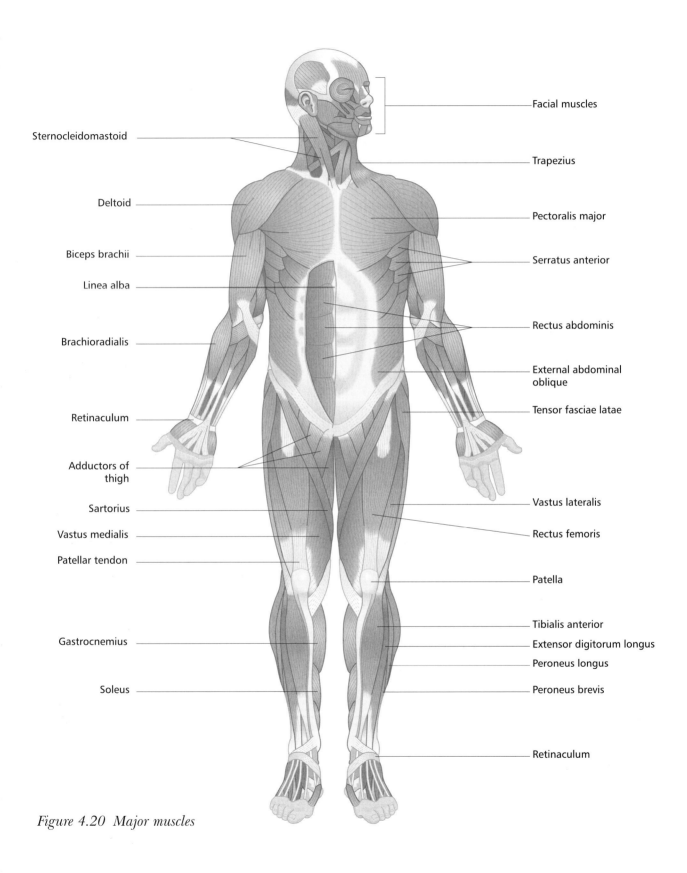

Sternocleidomastoid

Deltoid

Biceps brachii

Linea alba

Brachioradialis

Retinaculum

Adductors of thigh

Sartorius

Vastus medialis

Patellar tendon

Gastrocnemius

Soleus

Facial muscles

Trapezius

Pectoralis major

Serratus anterior

Rectus abdominis

External abdominal oblique

Tensor fasciae latae

Vastus lateralis

Rectus femoris

Patella

Tibialis anterior

Extensor digitorum longus

Peroneus longus

Peroneus brevis

Retinaculum

Figure 4.20 Major muscles

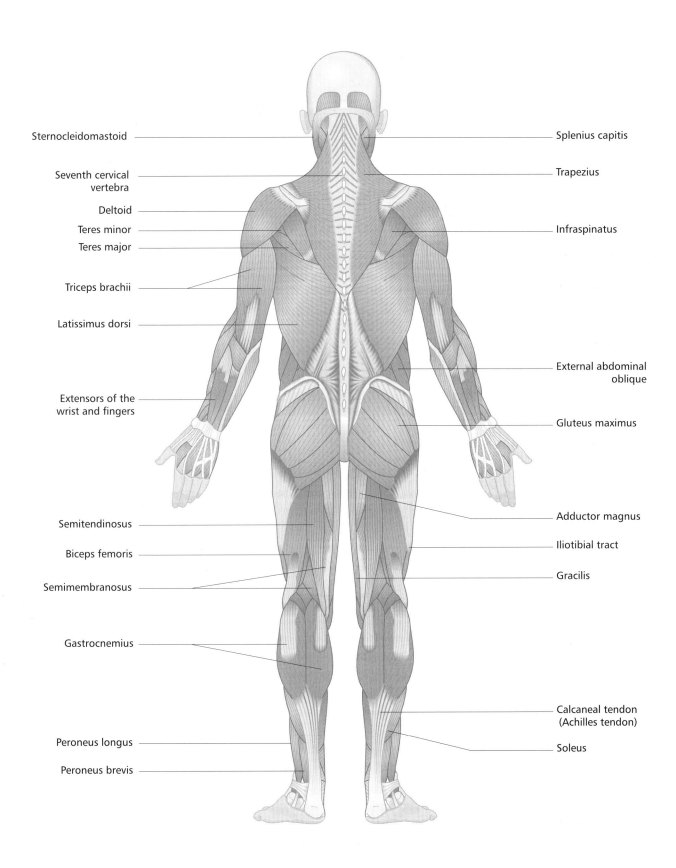

Sternocleidomastoid

Seventh cervical vertebra

Deltoid

Teres minor

Teres major

Triceps brachii

Latissimus dorsi

Extensors of the wrist and fingers

Semitendinosus

Biceps femoris

Semimembranosus

Gastrocnemius

Peroneus longus

Peroneus brevis

Splenius capitis

Trapezius

Infraspinatus

External abdominal oblique

Gluteus maximus

Adductor magnus

Iliotibial tract

Gracilis

Calcaneal tendon (Achilles tendon)

Soleus

Figure 4.21 A rugby player making a tackle would hold on to their opponent using the pectoral muscles

Figure 4.22 A sprinter will use the gluteals in the leg action of sprinting down the track

- Latissimus dorsi – the broad back muscle, will swing the arm backwards and rotate it inwards, e.g. when serving, a tennis player uses the latissimus dorsi to swing their arm back to hit the ball.
- Abdominals – these bend the trunk forwards and help to turn the upper body, e.g. abdominals are used to perform a sit-up exercise.

Pairs of muscles

The human body can perform a vast range of movements. To carry out these movements, muscles either shorten or lengthen.

Muscles work in pairs. As one muscle contracts the other relaxes. Muscles that work together like this are called **antagonistic pairs**. This type of action enables the body to move with stability and control.

Examples of antagonistic pairs are:
- Biceps and triceps – at the arm joint. As the biceps bend the arm by contracting, the triceps relax. As the arm straightens, the opposite occurs.
- Hamstrings and quadriceps – at the knee joint. The hamstrings contract and the quadriceps relax and the knee bends. As the knee straightens the quads contract and the hamstrings relax.

Figure 4.23

For example a long-jumper when driving off the board will use the quadriceps to straighten the knee joint at take off.

Agonist

This is the muscle that produces the desired joint movement and is also known as the **prime mover**, for example the biceps brachii is the muscle which produces the flexion movement at the elbow.

Antagonist

For movement to be co-ordinated muscles work in pairs so that control is maintained. The movement caused by the agonist is countered by the action of the opposing muscle called the antagonist, for example the action at the elbow caused by the biceps shortening is opposed by the lengthening of the triceps which act as the antagonist.

Fixator

This is a muscle that works with others to stabilise the origin of the prime mover, for example the trapezius contracts to stabilise the origin of the biceps.

Synergists

These are muscles that actively help the prime mover or agonist to produce the desired movement. They are sometimes called **neutralisers** because they prevent any undesired movements. Sometimes the fixator and the synergist are the same muscle, for example the brachialis acts as a synergist when the elbow is bent and the forearm moves upwards.

Muscular contractions

The following are types of muscular contraction:

- **Isotonic or concentric contraction** – this is when a muscle shortens and creates movement around a joint.
- **Eccentric contraction** – this is when the muscles lengthen when contraction takes place. It acts to control movement.
- **Isometric contraction** – this is when a muscle contracts but neither lengthens or shortens. During this contraction there is no movement around the joint. This is important when the muscle is acting as a fixator.
- **Isokinetic contraction** – this is a type of contraction where the muscle shortens and increases in tension whilst working at a constant speed against a variable resistance.

Levers

Levers are important in movement because they allow efficiency and force to be applied to the body's movements. Levers are made up of

Definition

Origin

This is the end of the muscle attached to a bone that is stable, e.g. the scapula. The point of origin stays still when contraction occurs. Some muscles have two or more origins, e.g. the biceps have two heads that pull on the one insertion to lift the lower arm.

Insertion

This is the end of the muscle attached to the bone that actively moves, e.g. the biceps insertion is on the radius.

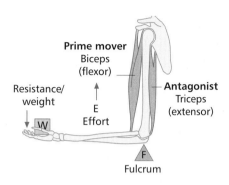

Figure 4.24 Lever system in the forearm

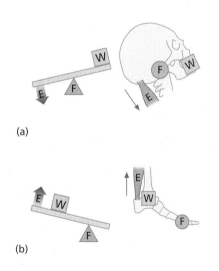

(a)

(b)

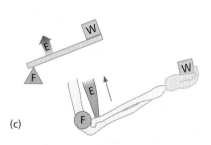

(c)

Figure 4.25 The three types of lever: (a) First-class; (b) Second-class; (c) Third-class

a lever arm, a fulcrum that is the pivot point, a load force and an effort force.

There are three types of levers:

- **First-class levers** – the fulcrum is located between the effort force and the load force on the lever arm, e.g. the neck joint.
- **Second-class levers** – this is when the resistance is between the fulcrum and the effort. If you rise up on your toes or plantar flex your ankles, then this lever is in operation.
- **Third-class levers** – this is when the effort is between the fulcrum and the resistance. This is the most common form of lever in the human body.

Energy needs for muscular contractions

Muscle cells burn carbohydrates and fatty acids when oxygen is present and this causes the production of **adenosine triphosphate (ATP)** that is essential for the muscles to contract. This process is called **aerobic metabolism** because oxygen is present.

If the process takes place without oxygen and only carbohydrate is used then it is called **anaerobic metabolism**.

The higher the intensity of exercise the more fuel, in the form of carbohydrates, is consumed. If the intensity is approximately 50% of VO_2 max, then fat is the main fuel used. As soon as that intensity is raised to 75% of VO_2 max, then carbohydrate becomes the major fuel source (see Chapter 3).

4.3 Cardiovascular system

The cardiovascular system transports oxygen around the body. Therefore it is a very important system for the athlete and coach to understand in order to improve performance. The cardiovascular system includes the heart, the network of blood vessels and the blood, which transports essential material around the body.

The heart

The heart consists of four chambers and is made from mostly cardiac muscle. The heart has two separate pumps whose main function is to pump blood around the body. The pump on the right-hand side sends **deoxygenated blood** to the lungs and the pump on the left-hand side sends **oxygenated blood** to the muscles of the body. A muscular wall, called a septum,

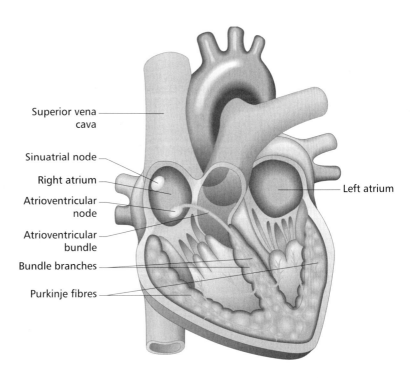

Superior vena cava

Sinuatrial node

Right atrium

Atrioventricular node

Atrioventricular bundle

Bundle branches

Purkinje fibres

Left atrium

Figure 4.26
The conduction system
of the heart

separates these two pump systems. The muscular wall of the heart is called the **myocardium** and is found between the inner **endocardium** and the outer membrane, the **pericardium**.

The two chambers at the superior (top) part of the heart are called **atria**. The two inferior (lower) chambers are called **ventricles**.

There are many blood vessels associated with the heart. The inferior and superior **venae cavae** bring deoxygenated blood from the body to the right atrium. The **pulmonary veins** bring oxygenated blood from the lungs to the left atrium. The **pulmonary artery** takes deoxygenated blood from the right ventricle to the lungs. The **aorta** takes oxygenated blood from the left ventricle to the rest of the body.

Like other muscles the heart requires a blood supply and this is transported to the heart via the **coronary artery** which brings oxygenated blood to the heart via capillaries. Deoxygenated blood is taken away from the heart and into the right atrium through the **coronary sinus**.

The heart also has **valves** which ensure that the blood can only flow in one direction. There are four valves within the heart. Two separate the atria from the ventricles and two in the arteries carry blood from the ventricles. The blood can only flow in one direction through the valves and this stops the backflow of blood. The blood that flows from the atria to the ventricles pushes the valves open; the valves are then closed by connective tissue called **chordae tendineae**.

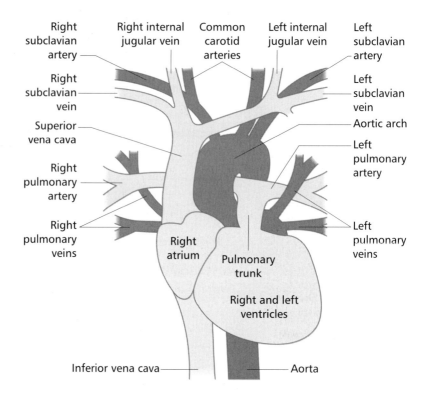

Figure 4.27 The arteries and veins of the heart

- **Atrioventricular valves** – a collective term for all of the valves between the atria and ventricles.
- **Tricuspid valve** – the valve between the right atrium and the right ventricle.
- **Bicuspid valve** – the valve between the left atrium and the left ventricle.
- **Aortic valve** – the valve between the left ventricle and the aorta.
- **Pulmonary valve** – the valve between the right ventricle and the pulmonary artery.
- **Semilunar valves** – the collective term for aortic and pulmonary valves.

The cardiac cycle

The cardiac cycle is the term that relates to the process of the heart contracting and the transportation of blood through the heart. The cardiac cycle is a sequence of events that occurs during one complete heartbeat, including the filling of the heart with blood and the emptying of the heart.

- Each cycle takes approximately 0.8 seconds and is repeated about 72 times per minute.
- **Stage 1 – atrial diastole** – atria of the heart fill with blood.

- **Stage 2 – ventricular diastole** – ventricles fill via the atrioventricular valves.
- **Stage 3 – atrial systole** – atria contract and all blood is ejected into ventricles; atrioventricular valves close.
- **Stage 4 – ventricular systole** – semilunar valves open, ventricles contract and blood is forced from the right ventricle into the pulmonary artery and blood from the left ventricle is pushed into the aorta. The semilunar valves shut and the cycle is completed.

Heart rate (HR)

The heart contracts and relaxes rhythmically, which produces a heartbeat. This is started by an electrical impulse from the **sino-atrial (SA) node** which is the 'pacemaker' of the heart.

▌▌▌*In practice*

Heart rate (HR) is measured by beats per minute (bpm). The average resting HR is 75 bpm.

A decrease in the resting heart rate is a good indicator of fitness. A trained athlete's resting heart rate falls below 60 bpm.

Figure 4.28
The cardiovascular system is very important for the athlete to understand in order to improve performance

Stroke volume (SV)

This is the volume of blood that is pumped out of the heart by each ventricle during one contraction. Stroke volume varies depending on:

- the amount of blood returning to the heart (venous return)
- the elasticity of the ventricles
- the contractility of the ventricles
- the blood pressure in the arteries leading from the heart.

Stroke volume is measured in ml per beat.

Cardiac output (Q)

This refers to the volume of blood ejected from the left ventricle in one minute. The cardiac output is equal to the stroke volume × the heart rate:

$$Q = SV \times HR$$

Cardiac output is measured in litres/minute.

Arteries and arterioles

These are blood vessels that carry blood at high pressure from the heart to the body tissues. The largest artery is called the aorta, and it leaves the heart and subdivides into smaller vessels. The smaller of these are called arterioles and have a very small diameter. The walls of arteries contain muscle tissue which enables the vessels to increase or decrease their diameter.

Definition

Vasodilation
This occurs when the artery walls increase their diameter.

Vasoconstriction
This occurs when the artery walls decrease their diameter.

The vessels can therefore help to change the pressure of the blood, which is especially important during exercise.

Veins and venules

These carry blood at low pressure and return it to the heart. Their walls are less muscular but gradually increase in thickness as they near the heart. The venae cavae enter the heart through the right atrium. The smallest veins are called venules and these transport blood from the capillaries. Veins contain pocket valves that prevent the backflow of blood.

Capillaries

These only have a single layer of cells in their walls. This makes them thin enough for red blood cells to pass through them. Capillaries occur in large quantities around the muscles and this enables the effective exchange of gases.

Blood and blood vessels

Blood vessels are an integral part of the cardiovascular system and are essential for the transportation of material around the body. During exercise, most of the blood goes to the working muscles so that oxygen can be delivered and carbon dioxide taken away efficiently and effectively. Blood consists of cells and is surrounded by a liquid called **plasma**. The average total blood volume in a male is five or six litres and the average blood volume in a female is four to five litres. Blood also consists of **erythrocytes**, which are red corpuscles containing **haemoglobin**.

> ### Definition
>
> #### Haemoglobin
>
> This is iron-rich protein and transports oxygen in the blood. The more concentrated the haemoglobin, the more oxygen can be carried. This concentration can be increased through endurance training.

4.4 Respiratory system

This system works closely with the cardiovascular system to ensure a supply of oxygen to the working muscles, which is so important in sports activities. The **external respiratory system** involves the exchange of gases between the lungs and the blood. The **internal respiratory system** involves the exchange of gases between the blood and the cells.

The term **cellular respiration** refers to the process that involves the production of ATP.

Nasal passages

Air enters the body by being drawn in through the nose. The nasal cavity is divided by a cartilaginous septum that forms the nasal passages. Here the mucus membranes warm and moisten the air and the hairs filter and trap dust.

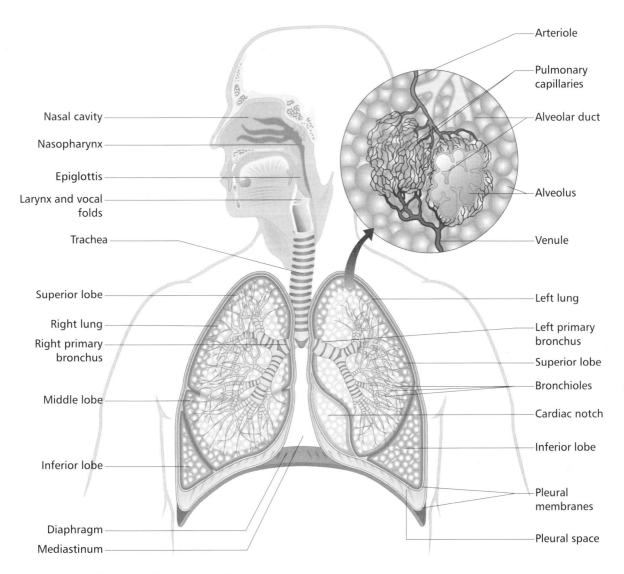

Arteriole
Pulmonary capillaries
Alveolar duct
Nasal cavity
Nasopharynx
Epiglottis
Larynx and vocal folds
Alveolus
Trachea
Venule
Superior lobe
Left lung
Right lung
Left primary bronchus
Right primary bronchus
Superior lobe
Bronchioles
Middle lobe
Cardiac notch
Inferior lobe
Inferior lobe
Pleural membranes
Diaphragm
Mediastinum
Pleural space

Figure 4.29
The respiratory system

The pharynx and the larynx

The throat has both the respiratory and alimentary tract so both food and air pass through. Air passes over the vocal chords of the larynx and into the **trachea**. Swallowing draws the larynx upwards against the epiglottis and prevents the entry of food into the respiratory tract. Food is sent down the oesophagus.

The trachea

This is sometimes called the windpipe. It has 18 rings of cartilage, which are lined with a mucous membrane, and ciliated cells which trap dust. The trachea goes from the larynx to the primary bronchi.

The bronchi and bronchioles

The trachea divides into two bronchi. The right bronchus goes into the right lung and the left bronchus goes into the left lung. The bronchi then divide up into smaller bronchioles. The bronchioles enable the air to pass into the alveoli where diffusion takes place.

Alveoli

These are responsible for gaseous exchange between the lungs and the blood. They are tiny air-filled sacs and there are many million of these in the lungs providing an enormous surface area (some have estimated the area to be the size of a tennis court!). The walls of the alveoli are extremely thin and are lined by a thin film of water which allows the dissolving of oxygen from the inspired air. The exchange of oxygen is illustrated in Figure 4.30.

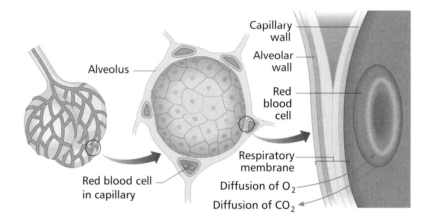

Figure 4.30 Gaseous exchange between alveolus and capillary bed

The lungs

These lie in the thoracic cavity, an area surrounded and protected by the ribs and the diaphragm and separated into two by the mediastinum which contains the heart. The pleural membrane that lines the pleural cavity surrounds each of the two lungs. The pleural cavity contains pleural fluid, which reduces friction by lubricating. The diaphragm borders the bottom of the lungs and is a sheet of skeletal muscle.

Breathing

Inspiration

Inspiration or breathing-in occurs when the respiratory muscles contract. These include the external intercostal muscles and the diaphragm. The external intercostal muscles are attached to the ribs and when they contract, the ribs move upwards and outwards. The diaphragm contracts downward and thus the area of the thoracic cavity is increased. The lungs are pulled outwards through surface tension along with the chest walls, which causes the space within the lungs to increase. The pressure within the lungs decreases and becomes less than the pressure outside the body. Gases move from areas of high pressure into areas of low pressure and so air is inspired into the lungs.

During exercise the **sternocleidomastoid** lifts the sternum; the **scalenes** and the **pectoralis minor** both elevate the ribs. These actions help to increase the size of the thoracic cavity.

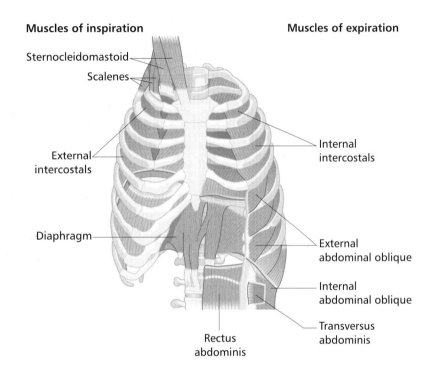

Figure 4.31 Muscles involved in respiration

Expiration
This is more of a passive process than inspiration and is caused by the relaxation of the respiratory muscles. When the external intercostal muscles relax, the ribs are lowered and the diaphragm relaxes. The area of the lungs decreases and the pressure within the lungs becomes greater than the pressure outside the body. Air is now forced out to equalise this pressure and expiration takes place.

Gaseous exchange

At the lungs
There is a movement of gases across the respiratory membrane because of the imbalance between gases in the alveoli and the blood. Oxygen moves from the alveoli into the blood and carbon dioxide diffuses from the blood into the alveoli. Athletes who participate in endurance events have a greater ability to diffuse oxygen because of an increase in cardiac output and an increase in surface area of alveoli.

At the muscles

This is a similar process. The high pressure of oxygen in the blood enables oxygen to pass through the capillary walls and into the muscle cytoplasm. Carbon dioxide moves in the opposite direction. When oxygen is in the muscle it attaches itself to **myoglobin**, which take the oxygen to the mitochondria and glycolysis takes place.

4.5 Short-term effects of exercise

The cardiovascular system

The following are short-term responses to exercise:

- **The heart rate** – there is a rise in heart rate which is designed to get the body ready for activity. This is called an anticipatory rise and is due to hormonal action. Then there is a sharp rise in the level of hormones due to stimulation from the sense organs and hormones. The heart rate remains high due to the need for physical exertion. Then there is a period when it remains steady and then it falls due to the withdrawal of stimuli and the drop in hormone levels. The heart rate eventually returns to its resting rate.

- **Breathing rate** – this rises due to the demand for more oxygen.

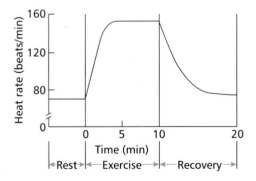

Figure 4.32 Changes in heart rate during sub-maximal exercise

The respiratory system

- **Tidal volume (TV)** – this is the volume of air either inspired or expired per breath. This increases during exercise.
- **Inspiratory reserve volume (IRV)** – this is the maximal volume inspired in addition to the tidal volume. This decreases during exercise.
- **Expiratory reserve volume (ERV)** – this is the maximal volume expired in addition to the tidal volume. This decreases slightly during exercise.

- **Residual volume (RV)** – this is the amount of air left in the lungs after maximal expiration. This increases slightly during exercise.
- **Total lung capacity (TLC)** – this is the vital capacity (see below) plus the residual volume and is the volume at the end of maximal inspiration. This decreases slightly during exercise.
- **Vital capacity (VC)** – this is the maximum amount of air that can be forcibly exhaled after maximal inspiration. This decreases slightly during exercise.

The following are **long-term adaptations** that may occur due to exercise:

- increase in bone density
- increase in capillary density and efficiency
- lower resting heart rate
- increased vital capacity
- increase in stroke volume at rest and during exercise
- cardiac output increases
- decrease in resting blood pressure
- Increase in haemoglobin, which helps carry oxygen; increase in red blood cells.

Effects of exercise on the muscular system

The following are the long-term adaptations of the muscular system after a period of exercise.

Aerobic adaptations in muscle:

- activities like swimming or running can enlarge slow-twitch fibres, which gives greater potential for energy production
- size and number of mitochondria increases
- increase in **myoglobin** content within the muscle cell
- onset of fatigue delayed because of higher maximum oxygen uptake (VO_2 max).

Anaerobic adaptations in muscle:

- activities like sprinting or weightlifting can cause **hypertrophy** of fast-twitch muscle fibres
- size of heart increases – called **cardiac hypertrophy**.

Tests to establish whether adaptations have taken place

Heart rate

Before exercise the pulse rate can be taken. This can be done using a heart-rate monitor, which can be used to assess the intensity of the training and to set goals to work towards. This useful device can also be used to record heart-rate patterns as the athlete exercises.

III*In practice*

A decrease in resting heart rate for a trained person
Cardiac output required at rest remains static as there is no increase in demand for oxygen. If the resting stroke volume increases, the heart does not have to beat as hard in order to produce the same cardiac output and therefore the resting heart rate decreases.

Cardiac output = stroke volume × heart rate

Breathing

Use of a spirometer will measure lung volume.

Anaerobic capacity

This can be tested by using a bicycle ergometer, a static bike with controllable intensity of exercise. Each subject performs a 30-second bout of exercise sprinting as hard as they can (called maximal exercise) on the bike. A computer linked to the bike records the peak power reached. The peak power is an indication of how hard the body can work for as long as possible. Those who have a high level of power are more anaerobically fit.

Blood pressure

This is usually measured at the brachial artery in the arm using a **sphygmomanometer**. This records the systolic pressure over the diastolic pressure. A typical reading for a male at rest is 120mmHg/80mmHg.

Weight

Energy balance is realised when input (that is, food eaten) equals output (that is, energy expended). When input exceeds output, then the excess energy is stored as fat unless extra activity burns it up. The simple answer to weight loss is to eat less and exercise more. We have already recognised the importance of a readily available supply of energy in sport, and so the right energy input must be maintained.

A common way of measuring whether you are the right weight is to calculate your **body mass index (BMI)**. Before a training regime you may simply weigh yourself and then re-weigh after exercise, but remember that your weight alone does not indicate fitness. Muscle weighs more than fat so training that increases muscle size is bound to result in weight gain.

Body mass index (BMI)

Your BMI is a measurement of your weight in kilograms divided by your height in metres squared.

$$BMI = WT (kg) \div HT^2$$

A BMI greater than 25 indicates that you are overweight. If it exceeds 35, then there is a severe health risk. A BMI over 30 for adults indicates obesity.

▌▌▌ *In practice*
BMI indicators
Less than 20 – underweight
20–24.9 – healthy weight
25–29.9 – overweight
30–40 – moderately obese
40+ – severely obese
There are problems associated with this type of measurement. Body composition is not taken into consideration so, for example, someone with high percentage of lean body tissue may well weigh the same as someone with a similar percentage of body fat. The measurement of body fat is more accurate, and techniques such as the use of skinfold callipers or underwater weighing can measure this effectively.

Progress check

1 Name the four main functions of the human skeleton.
2 Describe the synovial joint. Choose one such joint and explain how it functions in a sports activity.
3 Describe cartilage and what its function is in the human body.
4 Give an example of a sports movement that involves flexion.
5 Name three major muscles and describe their functions.
6 Give an example of a pair of muscles that work together. Say which is the agonist and which the antagonist.
7 Name and describe the three main levers.
8 Draw and label the main structures of the human heart.
9 Describe what happens to air as a person breathes in whilst performing a sports activity.
10 Give three short-term effects of exercise on the body.

5

Sports leadership skills

This chapter is an introduction to the skills, techniques and knowledge required when leading sports, recreational and play activities. The material in this chapter relates directly to Unit 5 of the BTEC First award and can be adapted to suit work with different groups and activities in the community. This chapter will help prepare students to lead practical sessions effectively. It is usual to practise sports leadership skills with other students before going out into the local community. Health and safety matters will be alluded to but these are covered in more detail in Chapter 2. This chapter will help to prepare students for the Community Sports Leaders Award as well as other related NVQ level 2 units.

Learning objectives

- To identify the skills and qualities required to lead a successful sports activity session.

- To enable effective planning for a sports activity session.

- To give ideas for effective delivery and review of a sports activity session.

5.1 Skills and qualities required to lead a sports activity session

Communication

There are many skills associated with being a good coach or leader of a sports activity. The skill of **communicating** with performers, other coaches and officials is very important if the leader is going to get the best out of everyone. Communication can be verbal or non-verbal. Effective communication also involves listening.

▌▌ *In practice*

Communication skills of the sports leader should include the ability to:

- *Be direct* – when possible make instructions brief and easy to understand.
- *Be clear* – avoid double meanings or confusion.
- *Separate fact from opinion* – be accurate in your analysis and leave emotion out of it.
- *Focus on one thing at a time* – too much information causes information overload.
- *Repeat key points* – this reinforces what you have said and helps to avoid misunderstandings.
- *Have a good sense of audience* – adapt your content and technique depending on the recipient.

Good communication when leading a sports activity should include the following practical aspects:

- Talk to individuals as they train. Make sure that they know that you are interested in them as individuals.
- Use positive comments rather than negative ones if at all possible, but do not give praise unless it is deserved.
- Ensure that you can control a group of young people by insisting that they respond to a signal, for example a whistle. Stress the health and safety aspect of this.
- Use your voice and vary your tone. Shout if necessary but not too often – call the group to you to give instructions rather than shouting.
- Use questions to find out what the group members know and understand.
- Try to make sessions fun so that motivation is high – but do not pick on individuals and embarrass them.

Organisation

An effective coach is well organised. Good organisation can relieve possible sources of stress and can ultimately help performance. Confidence in the coach is increased if the performer perceives him or her to be organised. Self-confidence on the part of the coach can also be increased if personal organisation is good.

To be well organised make sure that you:

- Plan well in advance and make the necessary arrangements for the activity to go smoothly.
- Prepare and organise the facilities that you will use.
- Prepare the equipment and check it for safety as well as for appropriateness. For example, is there enough equipment to go round the group – or is there enough for one between two?
- Work well with others who are sharing the leadership and develop a sense of teamwork – do you know what each of you is doing?

Figure 5.1 Effective communication with performers, other coaches and officials is very important if the leader is to get the best out of everyone

- Plan your session to take into account time, available facilities and the ability of the learners.
- Make sure you can change your plans if things do not go well or circumstances change. For example, have you made alternative arrangements in case the weather is wet and you cannot go outside?

Solving problems

The skills of analysing and problem solving are also important for effective coaching. You need to be able to analyse exactly what is going wrong, because then you are more likely to solve the problem. Analysis may relate to the skills that the learners are performing or their behaviour. You may judge that the activity needs to be changed because it is unsuitable.

Health and safety

To ensure that you lead a safe session that follows health and safety guidelines, make sure that you:

- Check that all the equipment is safe and in good working condition before, during and after the activity.
- Check that the facilities are safe. The playing surface must be free from dangerous materials such as large stones or broken glass. These checks should also take place before, during and after the activity.
- Check that the learners are fit and well enough to take part and that you have all relevant information about potential problems. For example, you may have a participant who is diabetic or asthmatic. Ensure you know the procedures to follow when referring health problems to someone who is qualified to deal with them.
- Always monitor the safety of the participants during the activity. For example, a game may get too rough and some learners may be vulnerable to injury – you may have to stop or modify the activity to ensure safety for all.
- Always have or have access to first-aid facilities. Make sure you know exactly what to do in the event of an accident or if there is an injury. If you are not qualified to deal with an injury, always get help from someone who is.
- Have emergency procedures and review them regularly.

See Chapter 2 for more detailed information on health and safety.

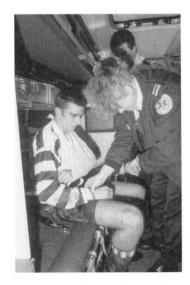

Figure 5.2 If you are not qualified to deal with an injury always get help from someone who is

Knowledge and skills required by a sports leader

Coaches need to have the skills to educate people regarding the following:

- **Hydration** – types of hydration, reasons for it and hydration recommendations before, during and after exercise.
- **Sports psychology** – including basic goal-setting that involves setting targets that are specific, measurable, agreed, realistic and timed (the SMART principle). Basic motivational principles including what motivates people to exercise and the difference between motivating children and adults.
- **Physiology** – including the principles of the warm-up and cool-down; fitness components – strength, speed, flexibility, power, agility and muscular endurance; the basic principles of strength – speed, power and endurance training; the principles of training – overload, progression, specificity, adaptation, variability, reversibility, recovery and overtraining.

Appropriate leadership style

The qualities of a good leader include being able to communicate effectively with other leaders and with participants. A good leader is enthusiastic and well motivated. It is easier to enthuse others if you appear to be enjoying your job as leader. Having good sports skills yourself helps particularly for demonstrations but is not essential. If you have a good in-depth knowledge of the sport then it is easier to gain respect. The standard of appearance of the leader is also important, especially when young people are involved. If you want the group members to be suitably 'kitted out' for the activity then it is important that you look the part and are appropriately dressed. You must always be **punctual** and **reliable**. If you wish your participants to turn up on time and to attend regularly then you must set a good example for them to follow.

A good leader is often charismatic, in other words he or she naturally commands respect because of their personality. A good leader will have a clear vision of what they are trying to achieve. Good planning and organisation is essential if you are to be a successful leader in a sports activity.

The leadership style that is adopted by a leader in sport depends on three factors:
- **The situation**, e.g. is the team winning or losing?
- **The members of the team/group**, e.g. are they hostile?
- **The personality of the leader**, is he or she naturally forceful?

There are many different styles of leadership, but the three most common styles identified are:

Figure 5.3 If you have a good in-depth knowledge of the sport then it is easier to gain respect

- **Authoritarian style** – this type of leader just wants to get the job or task done. They do not have a particular interest in personal relationships and they will make most of the decisions.

- **Democratic style** – these leaders are concerned with interpersonal relationships. The leader adopting this style will share out the decision making and ask for advice from other group members.
- **Laissez-faire style** – this type of leader makes very few decisions and gives little direction to the team. The group members choose what they would like to do and how they go about it with little or no input from the leader.

Most successful coaches, captains and so on, draw on a mixture of styles. A good coach may decide to be authoritarian when the team are losing but more democratic in training. In match situations, the leader may decide to let the team get on with it because interference might stifle the creativity of team members.

Coaching techniques

Depending on the situation, the coach should be able to incorporate a range of combinations of the following methods:

- **Whole, part, whole** – this is the technique of coaching a complete skill, then splitting it up into parts and then teaching it as a whole again.
- **Shaping** – this is a technique where reward or praise is given when the performers' behaviour/technique is correct. This **reinforces** the right technique and it is more likely to be repeated. The coach is therefore shaping behaviour (sometimes called 'operant conditioning').

A successful leader of a sports activity will also know how to give effective feedback.

In practice

Feedback

This can be given before, during or after the performance. Feedback is most effective if it is given just before or soon after the performance so that it is fresh in the participant's mind. Feedback motivates, changes performance or actually reinforces learning. The more precise the feedback then the more beneficial it is.

If the feedback involves praise or criticism or entails punishing the individual then this may change the learner's behaviour in the future. This process is called reinforcement.

Effective demonstrations

Copying or modelling can affect performance through four processes:

- **Attention**. To be able to imitate a demonstration, the performer must pay attention to it and focus on important cues (this is called cueing). The more that the leader is respected, then the

---

Definition

Reinforcement

- **Positive** – this is the giving of a stimulus to ensure repetition of behaviour, e.g. a badge for swimming.
- **Negative** – this is the taking away of a stimulus to ensure that the right behaviour is repeated, e.g. not giving any verbal praise if the individual performs the wrong action.
- **Punishment** – this is the giving of a stimulus to prevent a behaviour occurring, e.g. dropping the person from the squad for not trying hard in training.
- **Modelling** – this is a technique that involves using demonstrations or models of performance. The performer can see what is required and then try to copy it.

Figure 5.4 Demonstrations should be clear and appropriate to the participants' skill level

more likely it is that the learner will take notice of what he or she is doing.

- **Retention**. The observer must be able to remember the model or the demonstration. There must be clear demonstrations that also include understandable explanations and instructions.
- **Motor reproduction**. The observer must be physically able to copy the skill being watched. Demonstrations should therefore be matched to the capabilities of the observer. Your demonstration should be very basic for beginners and you should resist the temptation to show off your skills!
- **Motivation**. This is crucial as you want the learner to copy the performance. The use of praise and other rewards may increase motivation. It may also be relevant to insist on their attention, emphasising the need for them to watch closely so that they can copy your demonstration effectively.

Teaching/coaching styles (similar to leadership styles described above)

These can be adapted depending on the situation, the performer and the coach.

- **Command style (autocratic)** – the coach makes all the decisions and directs the performer and is authoritarian in approach.
- **Reciprocal style** – this involves group work where performers learn from one another.
- **Discovery style** – the coach takes a back seat and encourages the performer to discover solutions to problems. This approach may also be called **laissez faire style**.
- **Democratic style** – the performer participates in decision making.

Figure 5.5 Stabilisers on a bicycle: an example of mechanical guidance

Learning styles

These are the ways in which individual participants prefer to learn. Some learn better through instructions and demonstrations; others prefer discovery learning/problem-solving experiences. Some prefer to learn by visual means and some like to learn kinaesthetically or by doing rather than listening.

Guidance

The coach can adopt a variety of different guidance methods:
- **Visual**, e.g. demonstration.
- **Verbal**, e.g. instructions about technique.
- **Mechanical**, e.g. stabilisers on a bike.
- **Manual**, e.g. supporting a gymnast for a handspring.

Activities

In your session ensure that you include at least some of the following activities:
- Warm-up activities including stretching (must always be included).
- Games such as tag or relay races for fun and as a warm-up and also to satisfy the initial enthusiasm of the participants!
- Pairs activities – in order to practice skills without too much competition.
- Small group activities – to practice skills required in the team game if appropriate and to teach how to work with others effectively.

Figure 5.6 Support a gymnast: an example of manual guidance

- Minor games ('potted sports') – activities that may teach some basic skills related to running, jumping and throwing. These activities are also useful in teaching the participants how to respond to you – to your voice or the whistle.
- Skill circuits and fitness circuits – once skills have been learned you may include them in circuits to create some competitive pressure. This activity is also good for fitness.
- Full game activities – these should not dominate a session nor should you get into full games early on in your sessions. Many young people want to get into a game, but without the appropriate skills or strategies the game would be dominated by a few and no real learning would take place. However, there is also a danger of never getting into a game and leaving the participants feeling that they cannot see the relevance of the skills they have learned!
- Cool-down activities should always be included – as well as the physiological reasons for cooling down (see Chapter 3), this can be a useful way of calming the participants down. If they are school children whose next lesson is classroom-based, other teachers will be very grateful!

5.2 Planning for leading a sports activity session

In order to plan effectively for a sports activity, the following should be considered:

- age of the participants
- size of the group/groups
- use of other leaders or assistants
- skill level of the participants – what can they do already?
- what you are trying to achieve – be realistic! Record your aims for the session
- the facilities and equipment that you need
- time – what time do you have for the activity, including the introduction, warm-up, cool-down and time for changing both at the beginning of the activity and at the end
- health and safety factors including making a risk assessment, if necessary. (See Chapter 2)

Lesson plan

This must be realistic and be suitable for the level of ability of the participants (often called the target group).

The aims and objectives should be made clear at the beginning of your plan. Your lesson plan should also record any medical matters

Definition

Target group

This represents the type of people that you wish to concentrate upon for your activity session. For example, they may be:

- young children
- teenagers
- the over-50s
- mixed-gender group
- single-gender group
- those with specific learning needs.

relating to the participants. Take into account the number of participants, their ages and their gender. There may well be participants who have particular learning needs and you may find that a learning assistant will be on hand to help you. You should record resources and equipment used and the timing of your activities.

An effective lesson plan should form part of an overall plan or scheme of work. This scheme of work takes into consideration what is to be taught and what is expected to be learned over a period of time – normally a term or a year. The most important aspect of the plan is to state what you expect to be learned rather than just listing the activities that you wish to teach. Really effective planning also includes extension activities which can be given to those participants who are moving at a faster learning rate than others.

A good plan has a sequence of activities, for example: short introduction/warm-up/group activity/individual skills/pairs skills/small games/cool-down/recap.

In practice

Characteristics of a good session:

- *The session is lively but controlled.*
- *The session is well planned – has structure.*
- *The session has variety – try not to do one particular activity for too long.*
- *It fits well into what has been done before and what is planned for the next session.*
- *Participants are as active as possible – do not talk too much! A few words are often much better than a big speech.*
- *The leader checks regularly that the participants understand what is going on.*
- *A challenging and exciting environment – the facilities are appropriate and the activities are not too difficult and not too easy.*

Characteristics of a poor session:

- *There is too much talk from the leader.*
- *There is not enough action for the participants – too much standing around.*
- *There is no real purpose to the session – the participants do not know why they are doing what they are doing and the aims have not been shared with the group.*
- *Activities are too difficult or too easy.*
- *Lack of voice projection – they cannot hear what you are saying.*
- *Leader giving too much information at any one time – this confuses and demotivates.*

- *Lack of discipline – misbehaviour by the participants can lead to dangerous situations as well as being a barrier to learning. The leader must ensure control early on by insisting that they listen and that they do the activity as requested. Get help from someone else in authority if some participants are proving to be too difficult.*
- *Poor facilities/equipment.*

Health and safety

Make sure that you make a risk assessment of the activity (see Chapter 2). Check the facility and the equipment carefully. Ensure that you are aware of emergency procedures. Look out for any injuries and act immediately. First-aid resources should be well stocked and regularly checked. Make sure you know who to contact for help and where.

Legal responsibilities

Be aware of the regulations that are in place to protect both the participants and yourself as leader. Also you should be aware of the regulations that exist in the Children Act 1989, the Data Protection Act 1998 and the Activity Centre (Young Person's Safety) Act 1995.

Children Act 1989

The Children Act 1989 states that there should be a staff ratio of 8:1 for children under eight. Records must be kept showing the names of all employees and volunteers, and details of accidents and attendance.

There is an increase in awareness of child abuse and there are many positions of trust with children associated with the sport and leisure industry. This Act protects not only the children but also employees who may be accused falsely or accidentally of abuse.

You should note the following guidance (see also Chapter 2):

- Do not get into isolated situations with children.
- Physical contact must be minimal and involve only non-sensitive areas of the body, e.g. the hands.
- Use physical restraint only in emergencies.
- Show appropriate role model behaviour, e.g. do not swear, smoke or drink alcohol.

The Data Protection Act 1998

This Act makes it illegal to use information about individuals for any purpose other than that for which it was intended. Those that hold information must ensure its security and that it can only be accessed by authorised personnel. In the sport and leisure industry computer files often contain personal information on clients. The security of this information is covered under this Act. The control of data on such databases should be password protected and only authorised personnel should have access to the password.

The Activity Centre (Safety of Young Persons) Act 1995

Clubs and individuals must be aware of the above Act. They may wish to examine the activities they offer, particularly in relation to 'taster' sessions for people under 18.

The Act was passed in 1995. On 16 April 1996 the Regulations to the Act became effective. Since October 1997 it has been a requirement for all centres that want to provide the prescribed activities below, to be registered and licensed with the AALA (Adventure Activities Licensing Authority).

Licenses may be valid for up to three years, although most are valid for 1–2 years.

The prescribed activities are as follows:
- Caving (excluding visits to caves open to the public).
- Climbing (including gorge walking, scrambling and sea-level traversing).
- Trekking on foot, pony or mountain bike, on moorland or above 600m where it is more than 30 minutes travelling time to a road or refuge, and including off-piste skiing in remote country, but not on-piste skiing.
- Watersports – most activities involving unpowered craft (rowing boats are exempt) on any water where it is possible to be more than 50m from the nearest perimeter bank, or which is affected by tides or is turbulent.

The Act applies if the provision of the prescribed activities or level of activity involves instruction to those under the age of 18 in return for payment. If any one of these factors does not apply, then the activity – or level of activity – does not come within the scope of the Act and there is no need to register. Neither does the Act apply if the parent or legal guardian of the young person accompanies them throughout their participation.

Other providers must also be aware of the Act:
- Schools are exempt as far as canoeing with their own pupils is concerned.
- Local-authority owned centres: these are not exempt.
- Individuals who offer their services for payment: These are regarded as a Centre for the purposes of the scheme. If an individual freelance coach works for another person or organisation and is paid, however, and does not receive payment direct from the candidates, it is that 'centre' which must be registered – should the terms of reference apply – not the freelance coach.

(Adapted from British Canoe Union web site, 2004)

5.3 Delivery of the session and review

Summary

Much of this chapter has concentrated on the planning and method of delivery. The necessary organisational skills have been highlighted, including the need to adapt depending on different age groups, resources, facilities and equipment. Leadership skills have been covered and it has been established that a good leader will be flexible in their style of leadership. For example, if the group are a little hostile you may wish to adopt a more authoritarian style to maintain discipline. Later, when the group has settled into the activity, a good leader will then adopt a more democratic style using lots of questions and encouraging the learners to participate in their own learning.

Lesson plans are important and should include activities such as a warm-up and a cool-down. There must be progression so that there is always something new to learn. Competitive game situations should be avoided until participants have learned the skills appropriate to the game. However, games can be conditioned or modified so that only certain skills are practised, for example the one-touch conditioned game in football or the no-dribbling conditioned game in basketball.

Lesson delivery – the specifics

The leader should meet the participants punctually and make them feel welcome and at ease. The leader must then explain and agree the aims that it is appropriate for participants to achieve from the session.

The leader should check the participants' level of experience, ability and physical readiness to participate effectively and safely. It is very important that the leader makes sure that the participants have the correct equipment and clothing. If any participant is wearing jewellery for example, you may have to ask them to remove it for health and safety reasons. Remember that personal possessions remain the responsibility of the owner and not you – unless you state that you will look after something (which is not usually a good idea!).

The leader must include an appropriate warm-up and explain the value and purpose of this. Remind participants regularly about the health benefits of the activities and what is happening to the body when we exercise. The leader must be prepared to revise plans for the session if necessary. Flexibility is a sign of a good leader or coach.

Remember that explanations and demonstrations need to be technically correct and appropriate to the participants' needs and level of experience. Throughout the session the coach should check the participants' understanding of the activity.

Review

A good leader of sports activities will monitor and **review** or evaluate what they are doing and adjust their plans accordingly. Evaluation is the process of analysing the sessions you have planned and delivered. This can help in identifying what went well and what could have been improved.

Effective evaluation is essential if progress in coaching is to be made. Good sports leaders are always trying to improve what they do. This involves them thinking about and evaluating the coaching sessions they have planned and delivered, identifying strengths and weaknesses and learning lessons for the future. A technique for this is called the **SWOT analysis**.

Definition

SWOT

S – Strengths – What went well in the session? What good things came out of it such as positive attitudes and skills learning?

W – Weaknesses – What did not go so well? Was there any misbehaviour or lack of concentration by the participants? Was there confusion over what was to be done and were the facilities poor, etc.?

O – Opportunities – what could be done next time to improve? Will you make the activities more fun or more demanding? Could you get into a full game sooner? Are the participants ready for some more advanced coaching related to tactics?

T – Threats – What barriers are there for these opportunities? There may not be enough equipment to go round. You may not have the advanced knowledge necessary for more sophisticated practices. There may not be enough time to achieve what you set out to achieve.

The sports leader must also take into account this analysis in order to modify and develop coaching practice. The leader should regularly take time to learn about coaching skills and practice so that lack of knowledge is no longer a threat. This could include attending courses, conferences, reading journals or other relevant publications, observing and working with other coaches.

When evaluating coaching, it is important to also review the way the session was **planned**. The key to really effective coaching is to plan well; a problem during a coaching session could well have been avoided if more thought had been put into the planning process.

It is also important to take into account how the participants felt about the coaching session. Their views could be sought via verbal feedback or a written evaluation. It is important to record the results of evaluations by other coaches, supervisors, the participants themselves and also self-evaluation by the coach. The whole process is meaningless if the results are not acted upon. The elements of the coaching that have received favourable evaluations should reinforce good practice and that practice should continue and develop. The issues that come to light as a result of poor evaluations should be addressed and become part of an **action plan** to improve. Progress should be reviewed; personal action plans and coaching practice should develop and be updated accordingly.

In practice

Template for lesson plan

Name: .... *Date:* ....
Subject: ....
Group: ....
Activity: ....
Lesson objectives: ....

Phase	Learning points/Content	Equipment
Warm-up		
Early activity		
Focus		
Progression		
Performance/Game/ Summary activity		
Review		
Cool-down		

Progress check

1 List four points that will make a sports leader's communication more effective.
2 Make a list of things you need to organise before teaching a sports activity.
3 What health and safety aspects should be taken into consideration before leading a sports activity?
4 What factors affect the type of leadership style you choose?
5 What is meant by the whole-part-whole method of practice sessions?
6 How can a demonstration be fully effective?
7 Construct a lesson plan for a sports activity of your choice for a group of 11-year-old beginners.
8 What makes a session poor?
9 What is meant by a SWOT analysis?
10 Evaluate any sports activity session that you have experienced or taken yourself. How would you make it better?

6

The sports performer

This chapter covers aspects that sportspeople, coaches and leaders need to consider when trying to achieve the best sports performance. The chapter follows the requirements of Unit 6 of the BTEC First qualification. Sport-specific skills, tactics, fitness, diet, psychological factors and the demands of a competitive event are all addressed in this chapter so that readers can take these aspects into consideration when training, competing or leading in sport. The importance of goal setting, planning and evaluation is also explored so that learners can effectively plan, implement and evaluate their own programme.

Learning objectives

- To identify factors that affect sports performance.

- To prepare for effective training and competition in a selected sport.

- To be able to produce an action plan to improve performance and to identify evidence of possible progress in sports performance.

6.1 Factors that affect sports performance

The main factors that affect sports performance are:
- personal skill level
- tactics or strategies
- physical fitness
- diet and psychological factors such as levels of motivation.

The following factors may also affect performance:
- financial considerations
- effects of travel
- medical back-up, e.g. physiotherapists, sports therapists etc
- pressures and demands from others.

These factors will be explored using examples from a range of different sports.

Figure 6.1 The skills in hockey relate to dribbling and controlling the ball

Personal skill level

There are various specific skills that every sports performer must learn well. In hockey there are skills related to dribbling and controlling the ball. In netball there are skills such as shooting and passing, and in athletics the skills are throwing, jumping and running for example.

The word 'skill' can be used to describe a movement (for example shooting a basketball), but often we use it to describe the overall actions of someone who is good at what they do. Skills are **learned**. We are not born with specific sports skills, we learn them by watching others and by practising. So, to summarise, the word 'skill' is used to describe:

Figure 6.2 When a professional footballer performs a skilful pass he shows a technically good movement

- a specific task to be performed
- the quality of a particular action, which might include how consistent the performance is and how prepared the performer is to carry out the task.

For example, when a professional footballer performs a skilful pass, he shows a technically good movement, but the way in which he passes the ball has qualities that we might describe collectively as being skilful. This may mean that the movements are fluent, co-ordinated, controlled, goal directed (that is, aimed at achieving a particular target), efficient (no waste of energy and effort), consistent (successful most of the time), technically accurate and aesthetically pleasing (they look good).

Definition

Fundamental motor skills

These are very basic skills like jumping, kicking and throwing.

We learn these skills at a young age, usually through play. If these fundamental motor skills are learned thoroughly, they can be used as a base from which to learn the more complex actions required in sport.

Motor skill

An action or task that has a goal and that requires voluntary body and/or limb movement to achieve the goal.

Cognitive skills

These are skills that involve the mind or more specifically the intellectual ability of the performer. These skills affect the perceptual thinking and decision-making processes and help us to make sense of what is required in any given situation. They are essential if the performer is to make correct and effective decisions.

In practice

Jonny Wilkinson – the skill of kicking for a conversion in rugby

'My technique for the standing position is quite acute, more sideways – that's the most comfortable position for me. It allows me to get my hip into play, to get good rotation, to get a good swing into it that allows me to hit the ball further. Because I am not hugely tall with long legs, I don't have the lever power; my power comes from speed and whip of the kick.

There are three fundamental principles to kicking technique, which we call spot, line and follow through.

1   The spot is the focus on the point of the ball you're going to strike.

2   The line is the trajectory, the visualisation of the trajectory and a path that's already in play before you kick. You find a tiny point between the top of the posts and you aim for that and the line goes through the seam of the ball to that point.

3   Follow through is the line of the swing of the leg through the ball, not across it. The foot comes down, hits the spot on the ball and travels up the line that you want the ball to travel along. Therefore the foot and the ball are in contact for much longer. By doing that, you are totally in control of the ball.'

(Adapted from a newspaper article by Jonny Wilkinson. The Times, 7 October 2003)

Figure 6.3 Jonny Wilkinson uses his learned skills to kick effectively

135

Tactics

These are strategies or ways of playing, either together as a team or as an individual, that put you in a better position to succeed. There are attacking plays (for example in football) and defensive plays (for example zone defence in basketball). As a long-jumper in an athletics competition, one tactic might be to get in a safe jump early on in the competition in order to build confidence before really extending and trying for bigger jumps later on.

In practice

Arguably, Tim Henman is the master of net play in tennis. Henman has supreme technical skills, with an instinctive feel and touch for the ball, lightening reactions and superb athletic ability.

His tactical use of the net provides fascinating insights into his game and to how any tennis player could improve their tactical awareness.

Step 1 – Moving in to the net
Henman is always looking for the opportunity to move in towards the net. By anticipating a potential return he can get to the net quickly, making it more difficult for his opponent to pass him. Henman looks for short, weak balls, hitting the area around the service line. He anticipates his move towards the net when the ball appears to be dropping short and moves up the court to intercept the return.

Step 2 – Approach and return shots
Henman uses a range of approach shots, which follow a general pattern. Sometimes his approach shots are made down the line. The ball reaches his opponent very quickly, but at the same time reduces the angles available to him for the return. Henman carefully studies his opponent's play and plays return shots that he knows will cause problems for that player. This means that Henman uses a range of returns, including dropping the ball low and short or low and wide, towards the backhand of his opponent.

Step 3 – Positioning at the net
Instinctively Henman, once he has made his approach shot, moves towards the net. He tends not to head for the middle of the court, but aims for the same side on which he has just hit his approach shot. This is an important tactic as it reduces his opponent's ability to pass. Henman knows that he would expose himself to a pass down the line if he moved to the centre of the court after having hit the ball wide to the backhand of his opponent. Now stationed

at the net, Henman defends his position with his racquet in front of him and prepares either to move left, right or backwards, to deliver a lob.

Step 4 – Hitting the volley
Like many tennis players, Henman adopts a basic rule in hitting his return volleys. Henman will volley the ball back deep towards his opponent if the ball comes at him at net height or below. Henman returns the ball at an angle if the ball has come towards him higher than the net. Although he tends to follow this pattern, he understands the need to be flexible and will adjust his position to cover angles. In other words, heading for that side of the court where his opponent is about to hit the ball.

(Adapted from the BBC Sport Academy web site, 2004)

Fitness

The fitness requirements for a sportsperson are detailed in Chapter 3. The main components of fitness should be worked on and understood:

- Strength. This is the ability of a muscle to exert force for a short period of time.
- Muscular endurance. This is the ability of the muscle or group of muscles to repeatedly contract or keep going without rest.
- Aerobic endurance. This is the ability to exercise continuously without getting tired.
- Flexibility. This is the amount or range of movement that you have around a joint.
- Power. This is a combination of strength and speed.
- Speed. This is the ability of the body to move quickly.
- Body composition. The percentage of muscle, fat, bone and internal organs is taken into consideration. There are two main components: body fat and lean body mass (that is, body mass without the fat).
- Agility. This is how quickly you can change direction under control.
- Co-ordination. This is the ability to perform tasks in sport, for example running and then passing a ball in rugby.
- Balance. This is the ability to keep your body mass over a base of support, for example a gymnast performing a handstand on a balance beam.

In practice

Improving anaerobic and aerobic fitness
Interval training can help elite athletes to improve both **anaerobic** and **aerobic** fitness. To develop anaerobic fitness, an athlete will

work very intensely – running, swimming, cycling or rowing very fast – possibly above race-pace, before resting for a moderately long period then repeating the exercise a number of times, for example 10 × 30 seconds with 90 seconds rest. This is proven to develop anaerobic endurance. It is also possible to use interval training to improve aerobic fitness. By setting the pace and intensity of endurance training correctly – which requires scientific knowledge about an athlete's maximum heart rate and maximal oxygen capacity (VO_2 max) and the pace that is equivalent to – an athlete can be given a programme with equal work or rest intervals, for example one minute at maximum intensity followed by one minute's rest, which targets aerobic fitness extremely effectively.

For endurance athletes there is a limit to the level of fitness that can be achieved through steady-paced training, and for games players and the fighting sports like judo/boxing, interval training is useful because you can get quick results and effective improvement in endurance without the need for masses of volume, as EIS Strength and Conditioning Coach, Raph Brandon, explains:

> *'For a player on a mixed training programme where they have to work on strength, endurance and speed – like a rugby or netball player – during interval workouts, they can effectively improve their endurance in one or two workouts each week. Also, that is more compatible with their training programme because it removes the need for time-consuming runs or long cycles, which would interfere with their strength development.*
>
> *It's impossible to do interval training every day of the week, because it's too intense and the body would break down – maybe two or three high-quality workouts per week, integrated with a normal training programme.'*
>
> *(Adapted from English Institute of Sport (EIS) web site, 2004)*

Psychological factors

The way that we think and feel in sport has long been regarded as important to sports performance. Our own personality, our levels of motivation and arousal and our ability to cope under pressure and to concentrate effectively all influence the way we behave in sport. There are more details about psychological factors in Chapter 3.

'When the training is done and the big moment finally arrives, all athletes – no matter what their sport – must master their own fears in order to achieve their goal. The greatest barrier to success may simply be the fear of failure, leading them to 'choke' at a short putt or miss a penalty kick. It is vital to remain calm and in control. Psychologists recommend relaxing by exhaling gently to maximise concentration. Relaxation frees the mind from intrusive thoughts and sounds.

Australian golfer Greg Norman lost the US Masters in 1996 to Nick Faldo after leading by five shots going into the final round. Golf often looks deceptively easy to non-players, unaware of the mental and visual calculations made before any shot is taken and oblivious to the pressure that can break the golfer's vital concentration. The will to win can be the most difficult skill to master and can often be the difference between two athletes of equal ability.'

Adapted from the Science Museum's Web Text supporting its Science of Sport exhibition 2004. Reproduced with permission.

Figure 6.4 Mental and visual calculations are made before any shot is taken

In practice

Psychology and performance in various sports

In football, players use different methods to try to gain the psychological edge in order to enhance their own and their team's performance. Players can become over-confident when they anticipate an 'easy' victory and they often underperform. Or, if a team has just scored and the players relax their concentration, the opposing team can sometimes score a goal.

Winning athletes are able to blank out their surroundings and concentrate on the moment, ignoring distractions and the possibility of failure.

Tennis stars Bjorn Borg and John McEnroe were both great rivals and great champions. One was as cool as ice; the other psyched himself up by ranting and raving. Some rugby players heighten awareness by chanting and performing aggressive warm-ups which raise morale and heart-rate while lowering the confidence of their opponents. The chanting of their fans buoys up footballers. Teams generally win more matches at home and their performance is improved mainly because of this home advantage.

Figure 6.5 A good goalkeeper will watch closely as the opposition starts to build up an attack

A good goalkeeper will watch closely as the opposition starts to build up an attack. But a top professional keeper will analyse their positions and predict whether the ball will come from the left or right, across the goal or overhead. Psychologists say this is a natural, gut reaction. It cannot be taught and even the best players are unable to explain how they do it.

Top tennis or cricket players have great concentration as they prepare to play a shot. Their eyes narrow and their muscles flex in anticipation. They have phenomenal reaction speed and an ability to predict where the ball will land, which enables them to execute the perfect shot.

Adapted from the Science Museum's Web Text supporting its Science of Sport exhibition 2004. Reproduced with permission.

139

The best players react to what they visualise will happen. The latest research shows that the conscious part of the brain, the cortex, is very active as we learn a skill. We remember the best way to stand and where to position our arms and legs. Once a skill is mastered, the brain's automatic movement centre, the cerebellum, takes over. It seems that better subconscious control gives top professionals the edge over everyone else.

In practice

Mark Lewis-Francis and his 100m team-mates won gold for Great Britain, confounding the critics and beating the US team that were the odds-on favourites. Mark Lewis-Francis believes that any sprint race is won or lost far earlier than when the athlete settles into the starting blocks.

Lewis-Francis saw Linford Christie and Donovan Bailey as his role models when he was a child. He studied their technique to help him improve his running. He is a committed athlete and his life revolves around the gym, massages and physio work. Sprinting is one of the most competitive sports and he has worked hard to erase any negative feelings and improve on his mental strength.

Although he has good relations with the other competitors, they all look for an edge against one another. Lewis-Francis has learned not to be downhearted when he is competing against someone that has beaten him in the past. He uses mind games to try and unsettle less experienced athletes. On one occasion he competed

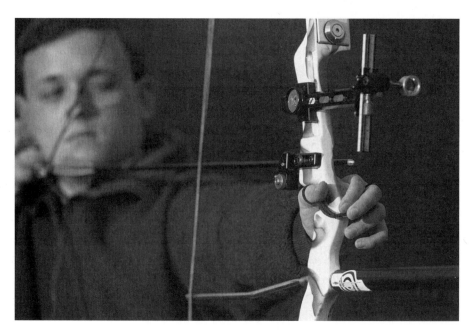

Figure 6.6 Better subconscious control gives top professionals the edge over everyone else

Figure 6.7 A sprint race is usually won and lost before anyone has got near the starting blocks

against Maurice Greene and was completely unsettled in the warm-up room. Since then he has vowed that he would never allow someone to psyche him out again. Some sprinters use aggressive tactics to psyche out their opponents, such as staring or jumping up and down in front of them.

Like all major athletes, Lewis-Francis suffers from nerves, sometimes shaking, particularly if he thinks about the huge numbers of people watching or the fact that he is racing against a world champion or record-holder. He now takes the antics of opponents like Maurice Greene in his stride and takes inspiration from the fact that Greene thinks he needs to try to psyche him out. Lewis-Francis resolves himself to just go out there, do his best and show the world who he is. He knows the whole sport is about beating his opponents and that is what he is there to do. Winning is as much in his head as it is in his body.

Adapted from the BBC Sport Academy website

Diet

There is more detail about the dietary needs of sports performers in Chapter 3.

Diet is a very important factor that affects sports performance. The content of your diet, when you eat in relation to competition or match days and so on, and the amount of fluid that should be consumed are all important in providing the best fuel for sports performance.

The nutrients that make up a good balanced diet are:
- carbohydrates
- protein
- fat
- vitamins
- minerals
- iron
- calcium
- water

It is important to eat sufficient fruit and vegetables in order to maintain a healthy diet. It helps to reduce the likelihood of coronary heart disease and some cancers. There are government guidelines that suggest you should eat at least five portions of fruit and vegetables each day.

Water is also a nutrient and is crucial for good health particularly for those who participate in sport. It carries nutrients in the body and helps with the removal of waste products. It is also very important in the regulation of body temperature. The body readily loses water through urine and sweat. This water loss accelerates depending on the environment and the duration and intensity of any exercise that is being undertaken. On average, individuals should consume about two litres of water a day. Those involved in exercise should drink more to ensure a good state of hydration.

See Chapter 3 for more details about dehydration in sport.

When exercise takes place, glycogen is broken down to glucose which supplies the muscles with energy. When glycogen stores are depleted there is less energy available and the athlete will become fatigued. It is recommended that carbohydrates should make up about 60% of a sportsperson's diet.

Glycogen is crucial for optimum energy supply. See Chapter 3 for more details.

Diets of sports performers

See Chapter 3 for details of the diets of sports performers.

In practice

Fuel for sport in winter

It is as important to eat a varied and balanced diet in winter as it is at any other time of the year. An adequate intake of energy, protein, vitamins and minerals is vital to maintain the immune system and prevent illness.

Carbohydrates

A good intake of carbohydrates prevents reduced blood-sugar levels and maintains muscle glycogen levels. This is important because low blood sugar and muscle glycogen are shown to be related to increased immunosuppression (that is, the immune system is suppressed and therefore unable to fight infection). Remember to refuel with a carbohydrate drink, cereal bars or sandwiches within an hour of training.

Vitamins and minerals

It is wise to maintain or increase your intake of fruit and vegetables over the winter months, particularly because some may not contain smaller amounts of vitamins than they do during the summer. Plenty of vitamin C from fruit and vegetables can help to ward off winter colds and flu, so aim for 5–10 portions a day.

Consumption of a wide variety of foods ensures that you have enough of the secondary nutrients such as zinc and selenium, which are also important in supporting the immune system. These are found in a range of foods such as meat, fish, eggs, nuts, milk, wholemeal bread and cereals. Athletes' requirements for some vitamins and minerals are slightly higher than the general population, but excessive intake of some can impair immune function and be potentially toxic – talk to the team doctor or nutritionist if you are unsure.

Figure 6.7 A varied and balanced diet is important

Protein

A good intake of protein is important in order to maintain muscle mass and to help you keep warm. Try out some hearty stews and casseroles made with plenty of vegetables, lean meat or poultry, or Quorn and pulses.

Fluids

It is tempting to think that you need less fluid in the winter compared with warm summer days, but even in the cold weather you should remember to keep up your fluid intake. You still lose a lot of water when training in the cold. All athletes need to drink 4–8 litres per day.

(Adapted from English Institute of Sport web site)

In practice

The diet of a top rugby league player

Brian Carney, GB and Wigan Warriors

Wigan Warriors and Great Britain international, Carney, has important dietary advice for staying in top condition, both during and after the season. He feels that breakfast is the most important meal of the day, particularly given the fact that he has not eaten for eight or nine hours. Carney eats a bowl of cereal or muesli with skimmed milk, having given up on full fat milk sometime ago. He takes a bottle of water with him to training, which normally begins with a weights session, after which he has a chicken sandwich. He then does training on the field followed by a light lunch. On the days preceding a match day he takes in carbohydrates in the form of pasta and rice to build up energy. Earlier in the week his meals would tend to be protein-based and he would avoid carbohydrates. Carney tends to opt for white meat and occasionally red meat for protein and drinks a protein supplement in the form of a shake, provided by his club.

Carney is very disciplined about his water intake, recognising that he needs to drink huge quantities of water to avoid dehydration. He feels that everyone should drink large amounts of water, even though he is often poked fun at for drinking as much as he does. His Wigan and British team-mate, Kris Radlinski, constantly ribs him about the amount of water he drinks.

Carney has given up fizzy drinks, which he used to enjoy, but last season, when he returned to his club for pre-season training, he discovered that his body fat was too high. He decided to give up fizzy drinks and now feels positively sick at the thought of drinking any. As another precaution he has also given up butter, which is something else he used to enjoy, but now he cannot eat anything, including sandwiches, which has butter in it.

For his evening meal Carney tries to eat a combination of protein and fresh vegetables. He is quite fanatical in trying to avoid any type of fatty foods. Despite this he does enjoy going out for meals and carefully combs the menu to make sure that he is not choosing a meal that could cause him difficulties in terms of fat content. As a professional rugby player, the club's conditioner allows a single day in the week for the players to eat whatever they want. Some choose junk food, but Carney avoids this. As the window day is usually a couple of days before a match, Carney tends to opt for a roast dinner in a pub and, every now and again he will treat himself to a pint of beer to help him relax.

(BBC Sport Academy web site)

Financial considerations

Many sportspeople, part-time as well as full-time professionals, now receive sponsorship, grants, appearance money and prize money. If you are serious about committing a large slice of your life to sport, it is important to consider all of the financial implications. See Chapter 1 for more information about sponsorship.

In practice

Funding young athletes

Unfortunately there is a limited amount of money available to fund young athletes. One of the few funds is the Ron Pickering Fund, set up by the wife of the late Ron Pickering in order to help rising young athletes. To obtain an application form, telephone 01438 715814.

The Reebok Challenge series of races is one of the few national-class, junior cross-country running competitions that offers prize money. Very few competitions actually offer prize money to the school age athletes who most need the funds.

The Reebok Challenge series offers £100 for a first place, £75 for a second place and £50 for a third place. Young runners can enter all 6 races and if they won the series they would be rewarded with an additional £250. The total potential prize money, assuming the runner wins all 6 races, is £850. This is one of the few prize-money competitions for young athletes and the problem remains that money paid to the top earners does not filter down to the youngsters.

(Adapted from BBC Sports Academy web site)

In practice

Lottery money decrease for sport

A fall in the sales of lottery tickets has had a drastic impact on the level of sports funding, even for those who attended the Athens Olympics. As an immediate reaction, the British government earmarked £14.1m to cover the shortfall, but this only went to the elite competitors preparing for the Athens Olympics.

The funding crisis was not expected to affect the current top athletes, at least in the short term. But it is the funding that was targeted to help rising talent that will fall.

On an annual basis Sport England distributes £200m of funds. In anticipation of cuts it warned the various sports organisations to expect cuts in their funding.

A Sport England spokesman said, "We are working on a worst-case scenario. We have warned them that there will not be as much to go round and that they will have to devise more economical programmes. We have to make savings and we don't want to get to a situation where we look in the pot and there is nothing there. At the moment there is no evidence that the current downturn will not continue."

These were wise words from Sport England, very reliant upon lottery money for funding. Their available funding fell from £268m during 1997/1998 to a projected figure of £170m over the period 2002/2003. They expect the figure to continue to decline as lottery ticket sales decline.

Sport England distributes funds at a grass-root level, thereby funding emerging talent. UK Sport, on the other hand, allocates £23m of lottery funding to elite athletes based on their performance. The Sport England spokesman said, "A lot of the money is forward-committed to future projects, but we have got to be careful that we do not over-stretch or over-commit ourselves. We have to take steps to keep the books in the black."

The then Sports Minister, Richard Caborn, said, "There is no doubt a drop in lottery revenue is damaging to sport. There is less money coming in from the lottery, and therefore into Sport England. But we are committed to maintaining funding at the same level in the run up to the Athens Olympics as was provided for the Sydney Olympics preparations."

(Adapted from BBC News web site, 2002)

The following is a list of funding planned by Sport England for world-class sports, 1997–2005:

- Athletics: £10.5 million
- Boxing £7.3 million
- Canoeing £6.5 million
- Cycling £10.9 million
- Gymnastics £8 million
- Netball £7.3 million
- Rowing £11.6 million
- Rugby Union £8 million
- Sailing £12.2 million
- Swimming: £10.2m million.

In practice

Rugby sponsorship: O2 extends England deal

The mobile phone network operator, O2, has entered into a sponsorship deal with the rugby world champions, England. The deal lasts for four years, beginning in 2004, costing the business £3m each year. O2 already had an ongoing relationship with the Rugby Football Union, which it has been supporting since 1995.

The deal secures sponsorship of the England official shirt until 2008 and the funds will also filter down to the grass roots, where the money will be used to develop young players. Former England coach, Sir Clive Woodward, said of the deal, "O2 has been a longstanding supporter of the England rugby team and has made a great contribution to the sport."

In practice

Turning professional as a surfer

The fact that Britain's top male surfer, Sam Lamiroy, comes from Newcastle just goes to prove that with dedication you don't have to have sports facilities on the doorstep to succeed. Most British surfers come from Devon or Cornwall.

Sam took up surfing at the age of 11 and most of what he learned in those early days was from watching good surfers. In fact no one told him how to paddle or perform on a board. After three years of self-training with friends, he became proficient and did not consider turning professional until he was around 20 years old.

Sam entered his first competitions at the age of 17 and to his astonishment he was ranked fifth in the world in the World Junior

Championships. Sam lacked funding and despite the opportunity to turn professional opted to go to university for three years. This bought him valuable time to take a long, hard look at the sport and, above all, to make initial contact with sponsors.

Sam was under no illusion that any sponsor providing money or equipment would want something in return for their investment. Sponsors tend to want a sportsperson or athlete to have attained a notable level of success, or it may be that the individual represents the type of lifestyle associated with their products or services. Sam quickly realised that he had to be a good surfer to attract sponsorship. He slowly built up his sponsorship, firstly at a local level and then at a national level.

Businesses such as those providing surfing products have sponsorship budgets. Sam prepared a brief background on himself and his competition results and sent it to all potential sponsors. He briefly outlined what he could offer and what he expected in return. Sam recognised the fact that he could not expect huge amounts of money or lavish gifts and began with t-shirts, watches, wetsuits and other surfing related equipment.

Sam adopted the gradual approach and over time he could ask for more sponsorship and get it. Once he began competing abroad he began to ask for a travel budget.

Sam recognises that any press coverage has a value. If a photograph or a feature about him appears in a newspaper or magazine he finds out how much that amount of space would be worth had he had to pay for it by placing an advertisement. He then gets a firm idea as to the value of the coverage he has achieved. He can then approach a sponsor and say that he has had £5,000 worth of coverage and ask for £2,000 worth of sponsorship. That way the sponsoring business feels that they are getting a good deal out of the sponsorship.

(Adapted from BBC Sports Academy web site, 2004)

Travel

As a sportsperson now or in the future, you have to get used to travelling. Some sportspeople on the professional tennis circuit regularly travel and fly around the world. Although this sounds glamorous and exciting it can be extremely stressful and can harm relationships with your friends, partner or family. When you find yourself in a different culture and climate you need to adapt to it so that your sports performance does not suffer.

III In practice

Preparing for the heat at the Athens Olympics 2004

The English Institute of Sport has built a room to recreate the Athens environment, calling it the heat chamber. The Institute studied Greek weather conditions for six years before the Athens Olympics 2004. With potential temperatures ranging from 34 to 43 degrees during the Athens Olympics, every possible preparation was necessary as heat has a direct impact on performance.

The heat chamber is capable of creating temperatures between four and 34 degrees by using a combination of heaters and air conditioning units. It can even reproduce altitude conditions of up to 3,000m by taking oxygen out of the air.

Most of the athletes competing at Athens had the opportunity to prepare in the heat chamber, including the runner Paula Radcliffe. When she broke the world record she ran at an average of 11.6mph. This performance took place in cool conditions in London and Chicago at around 10 to 11 degrees – a far cry from the temperatures in Athens. In such demanding conditions, athletes work hard to prepare for the effect of the heat and to reduce their body temperature before, during and after competing. The use of ice towels, ice jackets and other cooling equipment helps to achieve this.

In Athens athletes on average would lose 10 to 15 litres of fluid each day. This would need to be replaced at a rate of 1.5 times the loss. Re-hydration is crucial, not only to athletes but also to spectators and support crews.

The 2008 Beijing Olympics in China will see 95% humidity and the Institute has already begun research in order to replicate these conditions for British athletes. At the same time, work is underway to investigate the affects of cold in winter Olympic games and the impact of pollution on athletes.

(Adapted from English Institute of Sport web site, 2004)

III In practice

Use of ice jackets

Paula Radcliffe needs to cool off. So say Nike, who have developed the PRO-COOL Vest to stop Britain's big medal hope from boiling over while she warms up for her assault on the marathon and 10000m in Athens. According to the publicity spiel, the jacket 'slows the rise of an athlete's body temperature by 19%, reducing the risk of overheating and heat stroke and allowing the athlete a higher level of performance'. A Nike spokesperson adds: 'It's an

amazing fact but only 25% of our total body's energy goes into moving muscle while 75% is used to regulate heat.'
(Adapted from BBC Sport web site)

Medical support

All top-level sportspeople and many at a lower level have medical support for their training and competitions. Professional footballers have in-house physiotherapists and masseurs and the weekend footballer may well visit a physiotherapist because of an injury. There is a wide range of medical support now for sportspeople: chartered physiotherapy, sports therapy, sports massage, osteopathy, chiropractic, doctors, surgeons, podiatry, chiropody and complementary therapy.

Exercise and sports medicine is the medical care of illness in sport, giving advice about exercise programmes and also dealing with injuries caused by exercise and sport. Sports Medicine is not currently part of the NHS, so there is a limited amount of expertise available.

For information about alternative treatments see Chapter 2.

In practice

A day in the life of a sports physician who works for the English Institute of Sport

Working as a part of a multidisciplinary team is key to providing quality of service to the athlete, as Dr Rod Jaques, Sports Physician with the EIS in the South West, explains.

'During the course of a typical day, I would see six athletes during the morning for consultations and another six athletes in the afternoon, although it's not unusual to slot in a couple of athletes during a lunch break for brief consultations.

At least twice a day, I would meet with other EIS support staff – principally physiotherapists and strength and conditioning staff, to review the progress of particular rehabilitation cases. We must have excellence in communication with other members of the multidisciplinary team, otherwise we are simply not going to optimise the treatment for the athlete.

We work with nine sports, including track and field (so you can multiply that by at least another 10 to take into consideration all the various events!). About 70% of the cases I see are injuries, about 20% are medical problems in sport and about 10% are underperformance issues – people not *performing to their potential and wanting to find out if there is a medical reason for it.*

We have two other schemes in motion at Bath. Every fortnight, we have what we call a "case conference", whereby the doctor, physiotherapist, physiologist, strength and conditioning coach, the athlete's coach, nutritionist and psychologist – will get together to discuss an athlete's injury recovery if he or she is not making the anticipated milestones. With this full representation – where National Governing Body staff representation is also common – of seven professional disciplines the best brainstorming can take place on behalf of the athlete to optimise their treatment.'

(Adapted from the EIS web site, 2003)

Figure 6.9 There is a wide range of medical support for sportspeople (Photo from archive)

Pressure and demands

There are many different pressures and demands on sportspeople whatever their level of performance. Factors that can affect sports performance include family commitments and expectations. Training for sport can be a very selfish activity because you need to train mostly on your own in individual sports or with the rest of a team in team sports. This often means being away from home – an hour or two per week for the casual sportsperson and several weeks if you are an Olympic athlete preparing for a major competition.

Other team members can be very demanding not only with their expectations of you but also as competitors for places. If you are in a large premiership football squad you may be friends with other players. However, you often have to compete with them for a place in the team and this can cause friction and disagreement.

Coaches and managers can also be very demanding and their expectations may be unrealistic at times. It is important that you share your goals with your coach so that you agree what is expected from you.

Surrounded by sponsors, businesses and the media, there are many commercial pressures in sport. Many top professional sportspeople can often be distracted by the demands of commercial companies, so much so that their own sports performance may suffer.

In practice

The pressures on a tennis star

Anna Kournikova achieved fame by reaching the Wimbledon semi-finals in 1996. Since then she has given relatively poor performances on court, but nonetheless sponsors, the public and the media seem to have been obsessed with her. In 2002 she was knocked out in the first round of Wimbledon and it seemed for many that the world's love affair with the tennis player had come to an end. Her critics describe her as being arrogant, disinterested in tennis and sulky. She was interviewed on the day that she was knocked out by Tatiana Panova. It was a revealing interview. Garry Richardson asked the question whether she would consider stepping down to challenger tournaments in order to regain her confidence. Kournikova simply wanted to talk about the match and not the future. She was asked how she could regain her confidence, to which she replied that she would work hard to do that. She agreed that she needed to concentrate and that despite her game not being as successful as it had been, she refused to give up tennis.

Before the interview she was asked at a news conference whether her media career got in the way of her tennis career, to which she replied, "I don't think it distracts from my tennis. I am not involved in a lot of stuff. It is ninety-nine per cent less than what everyone says I do. Trust me – if I was not a hundred per cent committed to playing, I wouldn't be here."

Former Grand Slam doubles winner, Pam Shriver, commented on Kournikova, saying that she had a great coach and that she was desperate to regain her form. Shriver recognised that Kournikova was often unprofessional and that her attitude was not exactly

151

correct for a professional tennis player. Shriver was quoted as saying, "She is like that a lot of the time off camera. If you talk to people behind the scenes they will tell you that was the real Anna Kournikova. Right now I don't think she can come back. I think she is mentally shattered."

John Lloyd also commented on Kournikova's attitude. He felt that even though she was having a bad time in the sport, that she should accept this and that in any case she was still making a lot of money. She should also be able to handle difficult questions and media attention because she had always been willing to attract it in the first place.

Kournikova is one of the richest sportswomen in the world, having starred in music videos, Hollywood films, television, magazines and newspaper advertisements. Financially her career has been a huge success. But unfortunately all of these have got in the way of her ability to perform on the tennis court. Her latent talent is still there, having been able to win a singles title on the WTA tour. Perhaps it has come to a point with Kournikova that she is so successful elsewhere that she no longer needs tennis to underpin her career.

For many years The Sun newspaper carried a daily photograph of Anna Kournikova and despite her sulky arrogance, she remained a firm favourite with the public. In 2002, having been knocked out in the first round, her tennis career may have reached an all-time low yet her attitude to interviews could well undermine her media popularity and the adoration of tennis fans around the world.

She is no longer the seventeen-year-old girl that arrived on the scene, but she still behaves like a petulant teenager. Perhaps the world has finally lost its obsession with Anna Kournikova?

(Adapted from BBC Sport web site, 2002)

6.2 Opportunities to train and compete

Some have more opportunities than others to play sport, to train and to enter competitions. There are now fewer people participating in sport (see below).

Sports participation trends

(The following is adapted from General Household Survey (GHS) questions on sport – see Sport England/UK Sport, 1999)

The evidence points towards a real fall in the levels of participation in sport during the 1990s. Only those in the 60 to 69 age group experienced a significant and consistent increase over the period. All other age groups show some decrease. The decline in participation by 16- to 19-year-olds was particularly disappointing given the significant public policy commitment over that period by the then English Sports Council and its partners to increase interest and commitment to sport by young people.

The 1980s and 1990s saw significant increases in participation by **women** driven mainly by greater interest in keep-fit type activities including swimming rather than outdoor activities and traditional team sports. However, the profile of sports participants in England in the mid-1990s still showed significant gender differences, with men much more likely to take part than women. This trend is much greater in the **less affluent** North-East region than for example in the more affluent South-East.

A number of **ethnic minority** community groups have lower participation rates than the national average of 46% (people who had taken part in sport on at least one occasion in the previous four weeks). Only 39% of the black Caribbean and Indian populations take part in sport at this level of frequency while even smaller proportions of Pakistanis (31%) and Bangladeshis (30%) do so. Sport England's national survey of ethnicity and sport carried out in 1999 (Sport England, 2000) also showed that the gender differences in participation were greater amongst most ethnic minority groups than in the population as a whole and most marked in the Asian population.

The evidence on the **social class** of participants demonstrates that participation is significantly skewed towards the professional groups and that these social inequities have not become any less significant over recent years. In 1996 those classified in the 'professional' social-class group were still about three times more likely to participate in sport than those classified as 'unskilled manual'.

Sports clubs have the potential to play an important role in the provision of sporting opportunities. They can make the link between organised sport in school and sport in the community; provide the strong social ties that sustain participation into later life; provide opportunities for structured competition and performance improvement; and for those with the desire and talent they can provide the pathway into elite sport and high-level performance.

When young people leave school they tend to drop out of club sport. Around 47% of secondary-age young people are members of a sports club, but this drops to 17% among 16- to 19-year-olds and then continues to decrease further as people get older.

Sports clubs in England also significantly over-represent white, professional males and under-represent women (4% compared with

13%), semi- and unskilled manual social-class groups (3.5% unskilled manual compared with 16% professional), Asians and black Caribbeans and people with a disability (e.g. 13% of young people with a disability are members of a club compared with 47% of other young people).

The number of young participants aged between 6 and 15 may fall by 250000 between 1996 and 2024, and the number aged 45 and over will increase by 1.3 million. Overall, however, the participation rate is predicted to fall from 53% of the population in 1996 to 46% in 2024.

In practice

Against the odds

Gail Devers, US running star

US running star, Gail Devers, became interested in athletics when she was 15 years old. She was encouraged by her elder brother and soon learned to love the sport, setting herself a series of targets, which she sought to achieve. Like many athletes, Devers has had to cope with both illness and injury. In 1989 she was diagnosed as suffering from Graves disease. It should have been the peak of her career but it left her exhausted. Graves disease is a thyroid disorder and before it was diagnosed she believed that her athletics training was having a negative impact on her body. At her lowest point she even believed that her feet would need to be amputated, but with the backing of her family and her doctor she overcame the illness and won gold medals for the 100m at both Barcelona and Atlanta. She firmly believes that whether it's illness or injury, you have either to conquer it, or be conquered.

At an early age Devers got into the habit of setting herself personal goals. Each of these she writes down and determines to succeed in them no matter how long it takes her. She began her career primarily as a hurdler but has never won an Olympic gold medal. Nonetheless this has not put her off and she still strived to win that elusive gold.

Devers dedicates her life to her sport. She pushes herself in training and forgoes the normal life by going to bed early in order to make sure she has sufficient rest. She feels that if she works towards something and reaches that goal then this is what spurs her on to continue. Devers says, "Sport teaches you so much whether you aspire to being an Olympic athlete or not you learn about dedication, determination and a 'never give up' attitude. I am willing to conquer every obstacle that stands in my way, no matter how long that may take."

Figure 6.10 Gail Devers: 'I am willing to conquer every obstacle that stands in my way'

There are many opportunities to train and compete in friendly matches, leagues and championships. The following are encouraging participation and also giving opportunities to the best sportspeople:

- Specialist clubs, e.g. local hockey clubs.
- Schools and colleges – many have teams, and there are now schools with sports college status that have increased resources for sport. At the time of writing, sports colleges attract additional funding from a onc-off grant of £100000 and an extra £120 per student per year for four years. So not only do schools benefit through the raising of awareness of physical education (PE) and sport, but they are also financially rewarded, and that is why many schools are seeking to obtain sports college status. The Youth Sports Trust (YST) is responsible for the validation of a sports college.
- County, regional and national teams – most sports in the UK have these.
- Sports academies – there has been an increase in these in schools and colleges where elite young sportspeople can learn skills and become fitter for sport as well as following other courses such as vocational studies usually related to sport.
- UK Sports Institute (UKSI) – the aim of this organisation is to provide the best sportspeople with appropriate facilities and support. It provides sports science advice, coaching expertise and top training facilities. The UKSI comprises a number of centres located around the UK. Each individual home-country sports council has responsibility for the development of the UKSI in their area.

6.3 Action plan to improve performance and obtain evidence of possible progress

In order to monitor and evaluate performance, the following should be considered:

1 Assessment of current performance
   Factors which you need to take into account are:
   (a) Previous experience – what level have you reached in your sport?
   (b) Technical knowledge and skills – what do you know about your sport and what skills have you mastered?
   (c) Technical ability – what underlying abilities do you have?
   (d) Levels of fitness – what test results have you had related to all aspects of your fitness, e.g. cardiovascular/flexibility?
   (e) Commitment, training attendance and effort – how much time and effort do you give to your sport? How many times a week do you train and for how long? Do you keep a training diary?

(f) Access to equipment and facilities – do you have your own equipment for your sport? What facilities do you use? How easy is it to access training equipment and facilities?

(g) Access to effective coaching – who coaches you? How is this funded? How many coaches do you have?

(h) Diet – do you keep a food diary? Are there any foods you have to avoid? Does your diet vary depending on the stage of the season or leading up to a competition/match?

(i) Areas for improvement – having taken into account all of the above, what improvements could be made to enable you to be more effective in your sport?

(j) Methods of assessment – How do you assess your current performance/preparation in your sport? Do you use the assessments of others? Do you use video analysis or a coach's match analysis? Do you use a SWOT analysis (strengths, weaknesses, opportunities, threats)? Do you use objective tests such as a recognised fitness test or a psychometric test?

2 Targets for future performance
 (a) Targets should be based on the SMART principle.
 (b) Targets should be divided into short-, medium- and long-term, and seasonal.

3 Performance plan
 This should involve:
 (a) Aims and objectives.

Definition

Sports colleges

The Sports Colleges initiative is only one part of the Specialist Schools Programme introduced by the Government. Other specialist colleges include: Performing Arts, Technology, and Modern Foreign Languages. The programme is designed to give a distinctive identity to the school. Schools must develop partnerships with the other schools, the local community and with private-sector sponsors. The Government gives additional funding so that such specialist colleges can develop their particular area of interest.

The objectives of the Sports Colleges initiative are as follows (adapted from 'Sports Colleges', DfEE, 1999):

- *To extend the range of opportunities available to children.*
- *To raise the standards of teaching and learning PE and sport.*
- *To develop the school's identity.*
- *To benefit other schools in the area including primary and secondary schools.*
- *To strengthen the links between schools and private sponsors.*
- *To increase participation in PE and sport for pre- and post-16-year-olds and develop the potential of talented performers.*

(b) Recognition of resources required.

(c) Set and agreed goals.

(d) Training details and competitions.

(e) Diet details.

(f) Use of any technical equipment.

(g) Recognition of the barriers that need to be overcome. For example:

    (i) injury and illness

    (ii) weather

    (iii) travel and travel costs

    (iv) team selection

    (v) lack of equipment/facilities

    (vi) lack of coaching expertise

    (vii) financial implications to live and train

    (viii) the expectations and demands of others, e.g. personal relationships/family.

4 Monitor and evaluate performance

(a) Assess performance against SMART targets.

(b) Peer and teacher assessments.

(c) Feedback from coaches and training results.

(d) Acquisition of new skills.

(e) Recommendations for future plans/aims.

(f) Identify support needed, for example training courses, NVQs or other qualifications.

Evaluating coaching sessions

Evaluation is the process of analysing the sessions you have planned and delivered. As a sports performer you can also evaluate the performance of your coach – with their agreement of course! This can help coaches to identify what went well and what could have been improved upon.

Effective evaluation is essential if progress in coaching is to be made. Good coaches are always trying to improve what they do. This involves them thinking about and evaluating the coaching sessions they have planned and delivered, identifying strengths and weaknesses and learning lessons for the future. See Chapter 5 for more details.

See Chapter 3 for more information on preparation for sport.

Progress check

1 Give an example of a skill in your sport and state how you would practice it.
2 Explain an attack tactic in a team sport.
3 In your sport, what are the most important components of fitness and why?
4 What psychological factors should be taken into consideration when performing your sport?
5 In your sport what sort of food should you consume on the day of competition and why?
6 Give an example of sponsorship in three different sports.
7 How do athletes cope in a hot climate?
8 What do physiotherapists do?
9 What factors should you take into account when you are making an action plan to improve performance?
10 How do you obtain evidence on how well you are doing in your sport?

7

Work-based project

This chapter will enable you to identify, plan for and complete a practical work-based project. It covers the material needed for Unit 9: Work-Based Project. This chapter supports your sports-related work experience placement. Interview skills will be explored as well as documents related to applying for work, and you will learn how to record activities and evaluate them. During the placement you must complete a project, and you will find material in this chapter to help you.

Learning objectives

- To examine the skills needed for interviews for a sports-based work placement.

- To be able to use relevant documents for work applications.

- To be able to plan and carry out a selected project during the sports work placement.

- To be able to monitor, review and present the project.

7.1 The presentation of personal information

Your curriculum vitae (CV)

- Keep your curriculum vitae simple.
- It must be concise and straight to the point, do not waffle!
- It must be easy to read – avoid jargon. Make sure that it is typed and there are no mistakes.
- It must sell you – but do not try to be clever.

Your curriculum vitae must be tailored to the requirements of the reader. CVs are like adverts – your CV must sell you to an employer. You will be competing against other applicants who are also trying to sell themselves, so the challenge is to make your CV more appealing and attractive than the rest. This means that it must be presented professionally, clearly, and in a way that indicates that you are the ideal candidate for the job.

You must try to show that you possess the skills, experience and attitude that the employer is looking for. You will be judged by the way you present your CV because it demonstrates your ability to communicate.

The employer will have a good idea about what sort of person they are looking for and what sort of skills they require. Therefore your curriculum vitae should reflect the job description. The better the match the more likely you are to be called for an interview. Presentation and order is important. A well-presented CV indicates that you are professional, business-like and well organised.

You should aim to fit your CV on one side of A4 paper. A well-presented single side of paper will always make a better impression than lots of details spread over a number of sheets. Always try to use as few words as possible. Think carefully about the words you use – make sure they make sense. Never use two words when one will do.

In practice

In 2004 the Royal Mail postal service carried out a UK-wide survey by of Human Resource (HR) departments in large organisations. The following points about CVs were identified:

- *Incomplete or inaccurately addressed CVs and CV covering letters were rejected immediately by 83% of HR departments.*
- *55% of HR departments favoured CVs and covering letters addressed to a named person as opposed to a job title.*
- *Over 60% of HR departments said that the inclusion of a photograph with the CV adversely affected their opinion of the applicant.*

Once you have completed your draft CV, get another person to look at it and invite comments from them. Other people such as teachers, parents or friends may point out small errors that can be corrected easily. They may spot problems in the CV that you have missed.

Figure 7.1 Once you have completed your draft CV, get another person to look at it

Suggested curriculum vitae structure

Name
Personal details
Date of birth
Age
Gender
Marital status
Address
Telephone number (home and mobile)
E-mail address

Education and qualifications: institution – dates – awards (qualifications, e.g. GCSEs and first-aid awards/Duke of Edinburgh Awards) – grades

Work experience (other than the position you are applying for). Also include part-time jobs you have done, especially if related to sport.

Interests – show that you are interested in sport-related subjects and do not simply put 'socialising'.

CV covering letters

CV covering letters must be very professional and perfectly presented. Use a good-quality paper, ensure that the name and address are personalised to the recipient of the CV, and that the date is correct. Do not use scruffy photocopies – ideally do not use photocopies at all – CV covering letters should look pristine and tailored to the job concerned.

Look at what the job advert is seeking. Ensure that the key skills, attributes and experience required are reflected in the covering letter as well as your CV. Draw the reader's attention to the fact that your profile fits their requirements. Make the covering letter look like a special and direct response to the job advert and the personal profile that is sought.

Keep CV covering letters brief and concise. The reader will make assumptions about you from what you write, how you write it and the presentation of your covering letter.

Sample CV covering letter

Ensure you lay out the letter neatly and on good-quality paper, with your own address at the top right or centre top. Avoid fancy fonts and upper case (capital letters). Use one font (10–12pt size), perhaps in bold or underlined for the reference or heading if you use one.

Your name and address

Full name and address of recipient

Date

Reference if required

Dear (Mr/Mrs/Ms Surname)

(Optional heading, bold or underlined – normally the job title and/or reference if you are asked to quote one)

I enclose my CV in respect of the above reference (or state position advertised and when it appeared). You will see that I have the required skills, capabilities and experience for this position, notably (briefly state two or three attributes).

I look forward to hearing from you.

Yours sincerely

(Sign)

(And below print (type) your name)

CV covering letters for unadvertised positions or opportunities
It is all right to send a speculative CV to potential employers, that is, not in response to any advert. In this case you should get the name of the senior person responsible for staffing decisions in the area you wish to apply. (Telephone the company to find out the correct name and address details.) In these cases obviously you will not know precisely what skills they are seeking, but you should be able to imagine the type of person they might need. Here are some examples of skills or attributes (in your covering letter include two or three that best match your own profile and their likely interest):
- reliable and dependable
- decisive and results-driven
- creative problem-solver
- team player
- technically competent/qualified (state discipline or area)
- commercially experienced and aware
- task-orientated – you like to complete a job and have pride in completing it properly

- excellent interpersonal and communication skills
- sound planning and organisational capabilities
- loyal and determined.

Sample speculative CV covering letter

Again, ensure you lay the letter out neatly on good-quality paper, with your own address top right or centre top. Avoid fancy fonts and upper case (capital letters). Use one font, perhaps in bold or underlined for the reference or heading if you use one.

Your name and address

Full name and address of recipient

Date

Reference if required

Dear (Mr/Mrs/Ms Surname)

(Optional heading, bold or underlined – in this example you would normally refer to a job title, and include the word 'opportunities' or 'openings', for example: 'leisure assistant opportunities')

I am interested in any openings in the above area and enclose my CV. You will see that I have skills and capabilities that enable me to make a significant contribution to an organisation such as your own, notably (briefly state two or three attributes (skills) you have).

I look forward to hearing from you.

Yours sincerely

(Sign)

(And below print (type) your name)

As you can see, CV covering letters can be short and very concise and they need to be, otherwise people will not read them. Writing a short, concise covering letter for a CV also shows confidence and professionalism.

The bigger the job, the longer you can make your covering letter. Make your key points in a no-nonsense fashion and then finish.

Keep your CV and covering letter simple. They must be concise and easy to read. Your CV and covering letter must sell you, and must be tailored to what the reader is looking for.

Always keep copies of your CV and covering letters so that you can remember what you have written in case you are asked about them in an interview. Remember – never lie in your CV. This will get you into trouble if you get the job and someone discovers you have lied – you could then lose your job!

7.2 Interview skills

You may be called for an interview for your work placement and of course you will probably have an interview when you finally apply for a full-time job. There are many different ideas about how to prepare for an interview, but there are some basic tips that all interviewees should bear in mind.

Remember that interviews are a two-way process – the interviewer has every right to find out more about you and whether you are right for the job and you have the right to ask questions about the position and the employer. Some interviewers have better interviewing skills than others. It is well known that some interviewers make up their mind soon after you walk through the door and so **first impressions** really are important.

Types of interview vary considerably. There is no standard interview and many interviews develop according to the

Figure 7.2 Mock interviews are a good way to practice for the real thing

communication or interaction between the interviewee and interviewer. Interviews are not consistently successful at selecting the right person for a job, but they are still the most popular way of selection for a job. If you do get turned down for a job it does not necessarily mean that you interviewed badly. You may have been discounted because of the prejudice of the interviewer, for example you are too small/tall or you have a beard! Participating in a **mock interview** is a good way of getting some advice and practice before the real thing – but there is no such thing as a standard interview so be prepared for anything.

In practice

Things to avoid in an interview:
- *talking too much or too little*
- *yawning or seeming bored or gazing out of the window*
- *swearing or using inappropriate language*
- *sniffing*
- *fiddling with your ear/nose or any other part of your anatomy.*

Things to do in an interview:
- *be alert and seem interested (even if you are not)*
- *smile and be friendly but polite*
- *listen carefully – if you do not understand a question then say so*
- *answer the questions – try not to waffle*
- *be yourself – do not pretend to be someone you are not.*

The interview

Interviewers commonly assess interviewees according to their own personal style and approach – people like people like them. For example: friendly people like friendly people; results-driven people like results-driven people; dependable, reliable, passive people like dependable, reliable, passive people.

As an interviewee be aware that even the most objective interviewer – even if aided by psychometric job profiles and applicant test results – will always tend to be more attracted to applicants who are like them rather than applicants who are unlike them; it is human nature.

- Research the company as much as you can – products, services, markets, competitors, trends, current activities, priorities.
- Prepare answers to the type of questions you think you will be asked, in particular make sure you can say why you want the job, what your strengths are, how you would do the job, and what your best achievements are.

- Assemble hard evidence of what you have achieved in the past (make sure it is clear and concise) – proof will put you ahead of those who merely talk about their achievements.
- Have at least one other interview lined up, or have a recent job offer, or the possibility of receiving one from a recent job interview, and make sure you mention this to the interviewer.
- Make sure your CV is up-to-date and looks good, and even if you have already sent one to the interviewer, take three CVs with you (one for the interviewer, one for you and a spare in case the interviewer brings a colleague to the meeting).
- Acquire relevant material and read it: the company's sales brochures (for example a fitness club's leaflet on courses; a trade magazine, for example for leisure management, covering the company's market sector; and a serious (broadsheet) newspaper for the few days before the interview so you're informed about world and national news).
- Review your personal goals and be prepared to speak openly and honestly about them and how you plan to achieve them.
- Get into an enthusiastic, alert, positive mindset.

In practice

Preparation

Make sure you know:

- *where the interview is*
- *the time of the interview (punctuality is absolutely essential)*
- *alternative ways of getting there (in case the bus does not turn up!)*
- *who you have to ask for*
- *where you have to report when you arrive.*

Make sure you:

- *do not sit on the edge of the chair or slump in the chair*
- *do not wave your hands about*
- *wear something appropriate for the interview – get advice from friends, parents and teachers*
- *read what has been sent to you – there may be clues about what to expect in the interview*
- *get information about the job/company/leisure centre/sports club*
- *anticipate questions that might be asked and practice your answers*
- *Work out the questions that you want to ask.*

Possible questions at interview

- Tell me about your life at college/your time in your previous job.
  Answer: The question is an opportunity for you to demonstrate the qualities that the interviewer is seeking in the job, so steer your answer towards these expectations (without distorting the truth). When answering, emphasise the positive behaviour, experience and achievements (ideally backed-up with examples and evidence) which will impress the interviewer because of their relevance to the requirements of the job. The interviewer is looking for the same capabilities and behaviour in your college life (or previous job) that they want in the job. Your emphasis should be on your **achievements**, and how you accomplished them, and these should be relevant to the job requirements.

- What do you want to be doing in 2/5/10 years time?
  Or: Where do you want to be in 2/5/10 years time?
  Answer: Making a more significant contribution to whatever organisation I am working for. To have developed new skills, abilities and maturity. To have become better qualified in whatever way suits the situation and opportunities I have. To be better regarded by my peers and respected by my bosses as someone who can continue to contribute successfully to the organisation.

- Why do you want this job/work experience/placement?
  Answer: Reflect back the qualities required (see job requirements/specifications) as being the things you do best and enjoy. Say why you think the company/leisure centre/club is good, and that you want to work for an organisation like it.

- What are your strengths?
  Answer: Prepare three strengths that are relevant to the requirements of the job. Be able to analyse why and how you are strong in those areas. Mix in some behaviours, knowledge and experience as well as skills, and show that you understand the difference.

- What are your weaknesses?
  Answer: Acknowledge certain areas where you believe you can improve (and then pick some relatively unimportant or irrelevant areas). If you must state a weakness, the following are weaknesses that are also strengths: not suffering fools gladly; sometimes being impatient with other people's sloppy work; being too demanding; refusing to give in when you believe strongly about something; trying to do too much.

Other typical questions

- What was the last book you read and how did it affect you?
- Tell me about something that really annoyed you recently.
- Give me some examples of how you have adapted your own style of communicating to deal with different people and situations.
- Tell me about yourself.
- If you won a million on the Lottery what would you do?

7.3 The project

During your work experience you will need to collect evidence for a work-based portfolio or project. This evidence could include:

- placement logs or a diary of what has happened and what has been learned
- your observations of others at work
- witness-style testimonies from other workers who have seen you complete tasks successfully
- points for action, for example related to skills that you need to develop further.

Your project must list **key objectives**, **proposed outcomes** (what you think you will learn or find out), **timescales** and **resources**. Part of your assessment will also be on how you present your project to others. Identify how the project will benefit both you and the institution. If you want to get a distinction for this aspect then make sure that you:

- compare and evaluate the effectiveness of two different methods of presenting personal information
- evaluate the key objectives, timescales, resources and proposed outcomes for the project
- critically analyse the sports project, making recommendations for changes to future activities.

Planning

The key to completing a worthwhile work placement and project is good planning. The documents that you use (recording documents) should be written before the placement.

In practice
Recording information

- *Keep accurate and clear records of all information that you have gathered during your placement.*
- *Keep copies of your CV and job application/letter as well as notes of your interview preparation.*
- *Aims, objectives and proposed outcomes of your project.*
- *Travel arrangements and accommodation if relevant.*
- *Specialist clothing needed.*

Figure 7.3 You may need specialist clothing for your placement

The activities you choose to look at in more depth for your project should be carefully selected. Do not try to be over-ambitious. A project that is simple but well done is much better than one that is so complicated that you are unable to achieve what you set out to do. Discuss your choice of project with your employer. A project that may be useful to the workplace as well as for you will gain the support of your employer more easily and will also ensure that they help you with the information that you need. For instance, if your placement is at a gym your project may be about who uses the gym and what times are the busiest.

Figure 7.4 For your project, you may look at who uses a particular gym

Key outcomes

The key outcomes of your project may relate to specific areas of sport such as:
- coaching or training
- acquiring new skills or techniques
- sports coaching/leadership
- teamwork
- customer care
- health and safety procedures.

Skills

The skills that are needed and that you will acquire in your work placement should also be recorded and may include:
- practical skills, such as being able to erect a trampoline
- technical skills, such as knowing the right quantity of chemicals for a swimming pool

- people-related skills, such as being able to work at reception and helping the public
- teamwork, for example working with others to prepare a sports facility.

7.4 Monitor, review and present your project

Monitoring your project

Ensure that you write your achievements against your aims, objectives and targets. If your aim is to find out how the public uses the facility, for example, have you found this out? If you have tried to learn more about the industry you are investigating, again write down what you have discovered. You may also monitor:

- skills that you have learned at your placement
- activities you have undertaken – this may relate to coaching that you have undertaken.

Highlight methods of monitoring, for example interviews, witness testimonies, video evidence or tape recordings of interviews.

Review

This may take the form of a diary or a log of what you are doing and what you have achieved as you progress (formative review). At the end of your placement you may summarise what has been achieved (summative review). You may also record your strengths and weaknesses and the benefits that you have gained from your placement. Record your own career development and progression opportunities (what you hope to do next either as a student or in a job).

In practice

Personal skills

The work placement may give you opportunities to develop personal skills, for example:

- *practical skills of coaching or teaching*
- *skills related to numeracy, literacy or ICT*
- *clerical or administrative skills*
- *qualifications such as coaching awards or first aid*
- *personal qualities such as improving your communication skills.*

Presentation of your project

The way that you present your project will be taken into consideration for grading purposes. The better the presentation the more likely you are to achieve a higher grade.

The following are guidelines for a good presentation:

- Use the past tense. Record what has been done and what has been discovered, e.g. it was found that more females than males used the gym from 9.00 am until 1.00 pm
- Keep your writing simple and clear. Avoid long-winded sentences.
- Write in sentences and check for spelling mistakes.
- Make sure you read through your whole project and correct any mistakes – get someone else to look through it to check before you submit the final project.
- Use paragraphs. Paragraphs should be at least two sentences long but should never be longer than a page.
- Use lots of headings to break the project up and to make it easier to follow.
- Number the pages.

You may also be asked present parts of your project by different means, for example a short talk with a PowerPoint presentation could be included. Preparation is crucial if this is going to work well. Stick to the important points of your project and include lots of visual material – photos/video clips/leaflets and so on. Start with an introduction, including the aims and objectives of your project. Use graphs and tables if you have data to present, but again keep them simple and clear. Give your conclusions at the end and relate your findings to your objectives.

In practice

Visual presentations

- *Each slide should contain only the main points.*
- *Keep the font size large so that everyone can read the material easily.*
- *Use colours to highlight the text.*
- *Check spelling and grammar.*
- *Do not go on too long, and give the audience an opportunity to ask questions.*

Benefits of your project (to you and the institution)

Possible benefits for you:

- improved knowledge of sport
- improved knowledge and understanding of sports skills
- acquired new techniques in sport
- recognition of a career path, e.g. you want to be a fitness instructor and you realise what you need to do to become one
- identification of opportunities for progression, for example to do a higher-level course and then complete fitness teaching exams.

Possible benefits to the institution:

- You have created new materials for others, for example fitness record cards.
- You have written case studies (for example you have identified the benefits of exercise to the elderly) and these will be used in a gym leaflet/prospectus.
- You have done such a good job that there will be other work-placement opportunities.

Career pathways

After completing the BTEC qualification you may decide to progress to the next level and to stay in education full time or you may wish to study part-time and get a part-time job. Alternatively, you may decide to enter full-time employment at this stage. Ask yourself:

- What would I like to do as a job realistically?
- What do I need in terms of skills and qualifications to do that job? Typical jobs related to sport are:
- sports-centre worker
- fitness instructor
- sports coach
- sports development officer
- sports scientist
- professional sports performer
- sports groundsman
- sports therapist.

Find out the job descriptions for these career routes and the qualifications that are required. You are then in a good position to make a career plan.

Progress check

1 What makes a good curriculum vitae (CV)?
2 Why is a covering letter important?
3 Give five guidelines for someone who is going for an interview for a sports-related placement.
4 Write down four things that you should not do at an interview.
5 Identify what preparation you need for an interview.
6 Suggest a typical interview question and then write the answer that may help to secure the position.
7 How would you record information effectively for your project?
8 Identify how you would monitor and review your project.
9 Choose a career in sport and write down what qualifications and experience you need to get such a job.
10 What makes a good project presentation?

8

Practical sport

This chapter supports Unit 11: Practical Sport in the BTEC First Diploma in Sport. The focus of the unit is to improve the students' practical performances in sport as well as analysing the performance of others. This chapter is a summary of the BTEC specifications and provides general information to enable students to apply skills, techniques and tactics in a game or individual sport. Students must also have a good knowledge of the rules and regulations and the roles and responsibilities of officials in their chosen sports.

Learning objectives

- To be able to demonstrate, in your own sport, skills, techniques and tactics.
- To be able to identify the important rules, regulations and scoring systems in your selected sports.
- To investigate the roles and responsibilities of officials in your chosen sports.
- To be able to examine effectively the performance of other players in a selected sport.

8.1 Skills, techniques and tactics

Select sports that you will enjoy studying as well as playing. Choose two different types of sport.

Examples include:

- team: association football, basketball, cricket, hockey, lacrosse, netball, rugby league or rugby union, rounders and/or softball, volleyball, water polo (Figure 8.1)
- racket: badminton, squash, tennis, table tennis
- individual: athletics, golf, gymnastics, trampolining, swimming (Figure 8.2).

Figure 8.1

Figure 8.2

Skills

Applied to a range of sports, for example passing, receiving, shooting, serving, starting, striking, tumbling and rotating (Figure 8.3).

Techniques

Applied to a range of sports, for example different techniques of throwing, catching, dribbling, kicking, hitting, bowling and footwork (Figure 8.4).

Figure 8.3

Tactics

Including defensive, attacking, fielding, batting, set pieces, possession, penetration, communication, team formations, systems of play and marking systems, strategies, goal setting (Figure 8.5).

Record

For example, use of diary or logbook, video record, summary sheets, feedback from other participants, coaches, teachers and/or trainers.

8.2 Rules, regulations and scoring systems

Rules

Related to National Governing Bodies for team, racket and individual sports.

Figure 8.4

Regulations

Including player and participant, equipment, playing surfaces, facilities and safe practice, related to umpire/referee, timekeeper, lines person, starter and judge (Figure 8.6).

Scoring systems

Method of victory, method of scoring in specific team, racket and individual sports (Figure 8.7).

Figure 8.5

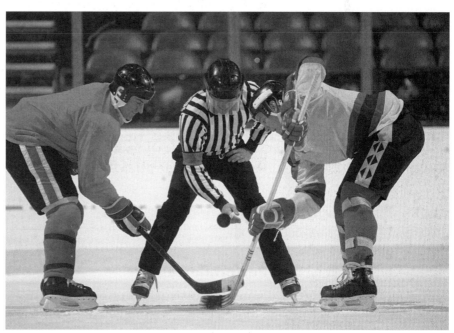

Figure 8.6

Figure 8.7

Figure 8.8

8.3 Roles and responsibilities of officials

Roles

For example, as an umpire/referee, scorer, timekeeper, table officials, lines person, starter and judge (Figure 8.8).

Responsibilities

Appearance, personal equipment, fitness, knowledge of rules and regulations, use of rules, control of game, safety of players/individuals, playing equipment, playing surfaces, fair play and spirit of the game.

Communication

Including use of voice, confidence, use of whistle, hand signals, decision making, interpretation of rules, terminology, scoring, starting and judging (Figure 8.9).

8.4 Performance of other players

Identify

Strengths, weaknesses, skills, techniques, tactical awareness, relevance to team, racket and individual sports.

Performance

Statistical analysis of performance, for example shots at the goal, number of interceptions, successful passes, misplaced passes, types of shots, number of skills performed and types of defensive or attacking play.

Figure 8.9

Analyse

Observation, discussion, recording systems, use of charts, tables and graphs, areas for improvement.

8.5 To get a distinction for this unit

Make sure you can:

- critically analyse your own performance and application of different skills, techniques and tactics, providing recommendations for changes and/or improvements in two different sports
- evaluate the use and application of the rules, regulations and scoring systems for play and/or performance as detailed in the appropriate National Governing Body guidelines for two contrasting sports
- critically analyse the performance of officials in two contrasting sports drawing valid conclusions and making recommendations for changes and/or improvements
- critically analyse the performance, strengths, weaknesses and tactical awareness of two athletes providing recommendations for changes and/or improvements.

8.6 Specific sports web sites

Amateur Athletic Foundation of Los Angeles (AAF). Supports Californian youth sports organisations and conducts youth sports and coaching programmes. Operates the Paul Ziffren Sports Resource Centre. Good sports web links, including SIRC, SportQuest, Yahoo Sport, Sporting News, WSF, BSSH and IOC. www.aafla.org/

BBC Sport. Online programme schedules with links, news, player profiles, audio and video highlights, discussion forums, results and search facility. http://news.bbc.co.uk/sport

British Gymnastics Association (BAGA). Founded in 1888; based at Lilleshall National Sports Centre. The only recognised governing body for UK gymnastics. Member of the World Governing Body for Gymnastics (FIG). www.baga.co.uk/

BUBL UK Sports Governing Bodies. Provides web addresses for a wide range of UK sports associations and organisations including: archery, athletics, badminton, baseball, chess, cricket, croquet, cycling, curling, fencing, football, golf, gymnastics, handball, hockey, lacrosse, mini-golf, netball, skiing, orienteering, polo, rugby, table tennis, tennis, volleyball. Also links to BOA, VEFA, FIFA and the Olympic Movement. www.bubl.ac.uk/link/s/sport/htm

Fédération Internationale de Gymnastique (FIG). Part of World Sport.Com. World governing body for gymnastics, and largest international sports federation, founded in 1881. Contains Federation News Archive, 1998 and World of Gymnastics magazine. www.fig-gymnastics.com

FIFA.COM. Fédération Internationale de Football Association (FIFA). Provides information about FIFA, the World Cup, football regulations, associations, laws of football, and has an International Football Hall of Champions archive (IFHOC). www.fifa.com/

Football Association. www.the-fa.org/

Football Task Force. Part of Department of Culture, Media and Sport site. Includes full text of report to Ministry of Sport, 'Football: Commercial Issues', 22 December 1999. www.culture.gov.uk/sport/default.html

International Association of Athletics Federations (IAAF). World governing body for athletes. www.iaaf.org/

Royal Life Saving Society. www.lifesavers.org.uk/

Rugby Football League. www.rfl.uk.com

Rugby Football Union. www.rfu.com/

Sportal. Huge European network of sports sites. Football, tennis, Formula 1, horseracing, rugby union, rugby league, cycling etc. covered with reports, live commentary, instantly updated statistics and good photography. www.sportal.co.uk

Sporting Life. Digital version of print magazine. Information-packed site, including instant news from Reuters, Sportal and other main sites. www.sporting-life.com

Sports.com. Provides European sports news, results and gossip. Good starting point, but more cluttered than Sportal. www.sports.com

SwimmersWorld.Com. provides news, e-mail updates, site of the week, coaching resources, Olympic News and Top 50 swimming sites. www.swimmersworld.com/

Swimming Teachers' Association. Founded 1932. Aim 'to preserve lives by teaching swimming, lifesaving and survival techniques'. www.sta.co.uk

SwimNews Online. Includes full text of Swim News magazine and archives from 1995. News, swimming calendar, world rankings, results and photograph library, biographies and links. www.swim news.com/

Glossary

Amino acids These are present in protein. There are eight amino acids that the body is unable to make for itself and these are called essential amino acids, for example leucine and threonine. The essential amino acids should be part of our dietary intake. The other 12 amino acids are called non-essential, for example glycine and glutamine.

Arousal This is a term used for the intensity of the drive that is experienced when an athlete is trying to achieve a goal. High arousal can lead to high levels of stress, both physiologically and psychologically.

Cognitive skills These are skills that involve the mind or more specifically the intellectual ability of the performer. These skills affect the perceptual thinking and decision-making processes and help us to make sense of what is required in any given situation. They are essential if the performer is to make correct and effective decisions.

Court games These games include tennis, squash and volleyball. Usually there is no contact between the players and a net separates the court, although in squash both players occupy the same space.

Cycles Coaches and performers often use specific goals associated with phases or periods of training and these periods of time can be split up into shorter-term goals. There are three recognised periods or units of time:

- **Macro-cycle** – this is the number of weeks making up the whole training period, e.g. 52 weeks.
- **Meso-cycle** – this is a set number of weeks to attain short-term goals, e.g. eight weeks.
- **Micro-cycle** – this is the short phase (usually one week) which is repeated up to the end of the meso cycle.

Extrinsic motivation This is the drive that is caused by motives that are external or environmental. The motives are either tangible or intangible rewards.

Field sports These are often associated with rural areas. Sports such as hunting, shooting and fishing are field sports and often involve killing animals (sometimes the prey becomes food for the hunter). However, the point of most field sports is the competition between man and the animal he wishes to kill. Many people who participate in field sports describe the 'thrill of the chase' as the most enjoyable aspect of this type of sport. Others oppose this activity and view it as cruel and unsporting because the animal has no choice in its participation and that the competition is not fairly matched.

FITT   F = Frequency of training (number of training sessions each week)
 I = Intensity of the exercise undertaken
 T = Time that the training takes (duration)
 T = Type of training that fulfils specific needs

Fundamental motor skills   These are very basic skills like jumping, kicking and throwing.

   We learn these skills at a young age, usually through play. If these fundamental motor skills are learned thoroughly, they can be used as a base from which to learn the more complex actions required in sport.

Haemoglobin   This is an iron-rich protein that transports oxygen in the blood. The more concentrated the haemoglobin, the more oxygen can be carried. This concentration can be increased through endurance training.

Hazard   Something that has the potential to cause harm.

Hypothermia   This involves a drop in the body's core temperature. If the core temperature drops to 35 degrees Celsius or below then you are deemed to be suffering from hypothermia. If the core temperature continues to drop then there is a real risk of death.

Insertion   This is the end of the muscle attached to the bone that actively moves, for example the biceps insertion is on the radius.

Intrinsic motivation   Inner striving to be competent and self-determining; a sense of mastery over a task and to feel a sense of achievement. (Martens, 1990)

Invasion games   The object of this type of game is to invade the opponent's territory as if you were at war with the opposition – which of course you are not! Rugby, netball and football are examples of invasion games.

Leisure   Free time in which there is an opportunity for choice. An activity, apart from the obligations of work, family and society, to which the individual turns at will, for either relaxation, diversion or to participate in new experiences.

Manipulation   The term 'manipulation' comes from the Latin, manipulate, meaning 'to handle'. It covers a range of techniques that use the hands to realign the structural system of the body, relax the muscles and improve circulation.

Motivation   A drive to fulfil a need. (Gill, 1986)

Energisation and direction of behaviour. (Roberts, 1992)

The internal mechanisms and external stimuli which arouse and direct our behaviour. (Sage, 1974)

Motor skill   An action or task that has a goal and that requires voluntary body and/or limb movement to achieve the goal.

Origin   This is the end of the muscle attached to a bone that is stable, for example the scapula. The point of origin stays still when contraction occurs. Some muscles have two or more origins, for example the biceps have two heads that pull on the one insertion to lift the lower arm.

Participation rates   This refers to the number of people within a group who are involved in sport compared with those who are not. For example, in a school the participation rates of girls in extracurricular sport could be 30%. In other words, three out of every 10 girls in the school are regular members of a sports team or club.

Personality   The sum total of an individual's characteristics that make him unique. (Hollander, 1971)

Personality represents those characteristics of the person that account for consistent patterns of behaviour. (Pervin, 1993)

The more-or-less stable and enduring organisation of a person's character, temperament, intellect and physique which determines the unique adjustment to the environment. (Eysenck, 1960)

Personality is an overall pattern of psychological characteristics that makes each person a unique individual. (Gill 1986)

Personality characteristics

- **Extrovert** – seeks social situations and likes excitement. Lacks concentration.
- **Introvert** – does not seek social situations and likes peace and quiet. Good at concentrating.
- **Stable** – does not swing from one emotion to another.
- **Neurotic** – highly anxious and has unpredictable emotions.

Recreation   An enjoyable activity that is refreshing and energising.

Reinforcement

- **Positive** – this is the giving of a stimulus to ensure repetition of behaviour, e.g. a badge for swimming.

- **Negative** – this is the taking away of a stimulus to ensure that the right behaviour is repeated, e.g. not giving any verbal praise if the individual performs the wrong action.
- **Punishment** – this is the giving of a stimulus to prevent a behaviour occurring, e.g. dropping the person from the squad for not trying hard in training.
- **Modelling** – this is a technique that involves using demonstrations or models of performance. The performer can see what is required and then try to copy it.

Risk   The chance that someone will be harmed by a hazard.

Risk assessment   Risk assessment is the technique by which you calculate the chances of an accident happening, anticipate what the consequences would be and plan actions to prevent it. (British Safety Council web site, 2002)

Saturated and unsaturated fats   Saturated fats are solid forms, for example lard, and are primarily from animal sources. Unsaturated fats are liquid, for example vegetable oil, and come from plant sources.

Sport   This involves competition between individuals or teams that is organised and includes physical activity.

Sports Colleges   The Sports Colleges initiative is only one part of the Specialist Schools Programme introduced by the Government. Other specialist colleges include: Performing Arts, Technology, and Modern Foreign Languages. The programme is designed to give a distinctive identity to the school. Schools must develop partnerships with the other schools, the local community and with private-sector sponsors. The Government gives additional funding so that such specialist colleges can develop their particular area of interest.

The objectives of the Sports Colleges initiative are as follows (adapted from 'Sports Colleges', DfEE, 1999):

- To extend the range of opportunities available to children.
- To raise the standards of teaching and learning PE and sport.
- To develop the school's identity.
- To benefit other schools in the area including primary and secondary schools.
- To strengthen the links between schools and private sponsors.
- To increase participation in PE and sport for pre- and post-16-year-olds and develop the potential of talented performers.

Sports' equity   This concerns fairness in sport, equality of access, recognising inequalities and taking steps to address them. It is about changing the culture and structure of sport to ensure that it becomes equally accessible to all members of society, whatever their age, ability, gender, race, ethnicity, sexuality or social/economic status. Sports equity, then, is more concerned with the sport itself. (Sport England web site, 2002)

SWOT S – Strengths – What went well in the session? What good things came out of it such as positive attitudes and skills learning?

W – Weaknesses – What did not go so well? Was there any misbehaviour or lack of concentration by the participants? Was there confusion over what was to be done and were the facilities poor, and so on.

O – Opportunities – what could be done next time to improve – will you make the activities more fun or more demanding? Could you get into a full game sooner? Are the participants ready for some more advanced coaching related to tactics?

T – Threats – what barriers are there for these opportunities? There may not be enough equipment to go round. You may not have the advanced knowledge necessary for more sophisticated practices. There may not be enough time to achieve what you set out to achieve.

Target games As the name suggests, the plan is to hit certain targets. This involves accuracy of judgement often called 'marksmanship'. Target games include golf and archery.

Target group This represents the type of people that you wish to concentrate upon for your activity session. For example, they may be:

- young children
- teenagers
- the over-50s
- mixed-gender group
- single-gender group
- those with specific learning needs.

The leisure industry The products and services associated with leisure activities.

Vasoconstriction This occurs when the artery walls decrease their diameter.

Vasodilation This occurs when the artery walls increase their diameter.

Selected references, further reading and web sites

References

Allport, G. W. (1935) 'Attitudes'. In: *Handbook of social psychology* (ed. Murchison C.) Clarke University Press, Worcester MA.

Atkinson, J. W. (1964) *An Introduction to Motivation*. Van Nostrand, Princeton NJ.

Bandura, A. (1976) *Social Learning Theory*. Prentice-Hall, Englewood Cliffs NJ.

Bull, S. J. (1991) *Sport Psychology, A Self Help Guide*. Crowood Press, Swindon.

Carron, A. V. (1980) *Social Psychology of Sport*. Mouvement Publications, Ithaca NY.

Chelladurai, P. (1984) 'Multidimensional model of leadership'. In: *Psychological Foundations of Sport* (Silva J. M. and Weinberg R. S.). Human Kinetics, Champaign IL.

Cox, R. H. (1998) *Sport Psychology Concepts and Applications*. McGraw-Hill, Boston MA.

Cratty, B. J. (1981) *Social Psychology in Athletics*. Prentice-Hall, Englewood Cliffs NJ.

Deci, F. L. (1985) *Intrinsic Motivation and Self-determination in Human Behaviour*. Plenum Press, New York.

Dweck, A. S. (1980) *Learned Helplessness in Sport*. Human Kinetics, Champaign IL.

Eysenck, H. J. (1960) *The Structure and Measurement of Personality*. Routledge, London.

Gill, D. L. (1986) *Psychological Dynamics of Sport*. Human Kinetics, Champaign IL.

Hinkle, J. S. *et al.* (1989) 'Running behaviour'. *Journal of Sport Behaviour*, 15, 263–277.

Hollander, E.R. (1971) *Principles and Methods of Social Psychology*, 2nd edn. Oxford University Press, New York.

Honeybourne, J. (2003) *BTEC National Sport*. Nelson Thornes Ltd, Cheltenham.

Honeybourne, J. *et al.* (2004) *Advanced PE and Sport*. Nelson Thornes Ltd, Cheltenham.

Honeybourne, J. M., Hill M. and Wyse J. (1998) *PE for You*. Nelson Thornes Ltd, Cheltenham.

Hull, C. L. (1943) *Principles of Behaviour.* Appleton-Century-Crofts, New York.

Kroll, W. *et al.* (1998). 'Multivariate personality profile analysis of four athletic groups'. In Cox, R. *Sport Psychology.* WCB/ McGraw-Hill, Boston MA.

Locke, E. A., and Latham, G. P. (1985) 'The application of goal setting to sports'. *Journal of Sports Psychology*, 7, 205–222.

Martens, R., Vealey, R. S., Burton D. (1990) *Competitive Anxiety in Sport.* Human Kinetics, Champaign IL.

Mosston, M. and Ashworth S. (1986) *Teaching Physical Education.* Merrill, Colombus OH.

Pervin, L. (1993) *Personality Theory and Research.* Wiley, New York.

Robb, M. (1972) *The Dynamics of Skill Acquisition.* Prentice-Hall, Englewood Cliffs NJ.

Roberts, G. C. (ed) (1992) *Motivation in Sport and Exercise.* Human Kinetics, Champaign IL.

Sage, G. H. (1974) *Sport and American Society.* Addison-Wesley, Boston MA.

Schmidt, R. A. (1991) *Motor Learning and Performance.* Human Kinetics, Champaign IL.

Sharp, R. (1992) *Acquiring Skill in Sport.* Sports Dynamics, Eastbourne.

Silva, J. M., Weinberg, R. S. (ed) (1984) *Psychological Foundations of Sport.* Human Kinetics, Champaign IL.

Skinner, B. F. (1953) *Science and Human Behaviour.* Macmillan, New York.

Triandis, H. C. (1977) *Interpersonal Behaviour.* Brooks/Cole, Monterey CA.

Weinberg, R. S. (1984) 'The relationship between extrinsic rewards and intrinsic motivation'. In: Silva J.M. and Weinberg R.S. *Psychological Foundations of Sport.* Human Kinetics, Champaign IL.

Willis, J. D. and Campbell L. F. (1992) *Exercise Psychology.* Human Kinetics, Champaign IL.

Wood, B. (1998) Applying Psychology to Sport, Hodder & Stoughton, London.

Yerkes, R. M. and Dodson J. D. (1908) 'The relation of strength of stimulus to rapidity of habit formation'. *Journal of Neurological Psychology.*

Web sites

Active for Life. Fitness programmes aimed at adults aged 16 and over. Can fill in an activity analyser which provides personalised information and suggestions for activity. Links to other useful sites. www.active.org.uk/

American Alliance for Health, Physical Education, Recreation and Dance (AAHPERD). www.aahperd.org/

BBC Sport web site 2004. www.news.bbc.co.uk/sport

British Association of Advisers and Lecturers in Physical Education (BAALPE). Association for advisers, lecturers, inspectors, consultants, advisory teachers and other professionals with qualifications in PE, sport and dance. Holds annual conference in July. www.baalpc.org/

British Canoe Union. www.bcu.org.uk

British Heart Foundation. Charity which aims to play a role in the fight against heart disease. Includes sections for children under 12, young people, teachers and youth workers. Contains glossary of heart-related terminology and publications section. www.bhf. org.uk

British Olympic Association. Responsible for sending Team Great Britain to Olympic Games and managing the team. Provides information about BOA School programme, School Olympic Camps, Youth Olympic Challenge competition. Downloadable file of 'The Olympic Spirit in the New Millennium pack, and information about Summer and Winter Sports'. www.olympics. org.uk

British Safety Council web site 2004. www.britishsafetycouncil.co.uk

Canadian Association for Health, Physical Education, Recreation and Dance (CAHPERD). www.cahperd.ca

Central Council for Physical Recreation (CCPR). www.ccpr.org.uk

Commission for Racial Equality. www.cre.gov.uk

Commonwealth Games 2002. Web site of Manchester 2000, the XVII games. Provides games venues, sports programme and key data about games. www.commonwealthgames.com

Department for Education and Skills www.dfes.gov.uk

Department for the Environment, Food and Rural Affairs. www.defra. gov.uk

Department of Health. www.doh.gov.uk

Department of Health, Health Survey for England. The health of young people 1995–1997. Includes section on physical activity of those aged 2–24. www.official-documents.co.uk

DfEE Physical Education. Physical education web site maintained by PEAUK and BAALPE. www.pea.uk.com

English Federation of Disability Sport. www.efds.co.uk

English Institute of Sport (EIS). www.eis2win.co.uk

Health Development Agency web site 2004. www.hda-online.org.uk/

Institute of Youth Sport Trust. UK's first dedicated research and development centre for youth sport, established as a partnership between the Youth Sport Trust and Loughborough University. www.youthsport.net/iys/index.cfm

International Council of Sport Science and Physical Education. (ICSSPE)/Conseil Internationale pour l'Education Physique et la Science du Sport (CIEPSS). In English, French, German and Spanish. Has 200 member organisations from 60 nations, including governing bodies, international sport and sport science organisations, non-governmental organisations (NGOs) and university/research centres. Works in formal associate relations with UNESCO, IOC and WHO. Produces scientific research publications, bulletins and newsletters, and organises the Pre-Olympic Scientific Conference every four years. ICSSPE held World Summit on Physical Education in November 1999 (Berlin) and Pre-Olympic Congress, 'International Congress on Sports Science, Sports Medicine and Physical Education', in September 2000 (Brisbane). www.icsspe.org/

International Olympic Committee. Has links to the Olympic Museum, International Sports Federations, National Olympic Committees, Sydney 2000 Olympics, Salt Lake 2002, Athens 2004, and Olympic Television Archive Bureau (OTAB). www.olympic.org/

International Society for Comparative Physical Education and Sport (ISCPES). Founded 1978. Holds conferences every two years. ISCPES is a research and educational organisation whose mission is to initiate and strengthen research and teaching in comparative physical education and sport around the world. www.iscpes.org

National Council for School Sport. www.schoolsport.freeserve.co.uk

National Curriculum for Physical Education. On main DfEE National Curriculum web site. Files may be downloaded to disk. Includes key stage 3 and 4, and covers the main areas: Games, Gymnastic Activities, Dance; Athletic Activities, Outdoor and Adventurous Activities, Swimming. www.nc.uk.net

National Playing Fields Association. www.npfa.co.uk

Physical Education Association of the United Kingdom (PEAUK). The lead body for PE in the UK, representing interests of around 4000 members, of which 3000 are serving teachers. Founded in 1899 as the Ling Association, its objective is to promote the improvement of the physical health of the community through physical education, health education and recreation. Provides information about vacancies, conferences and courses, and British Journal of Physical Education. A gateway to Teleschool, AAHPERD, CAHPERD, ICSSPE, ASCA, Virtual School and Sports Media. Recommended sports links include World Wide Web of Sports, Olympic Movement, SPORTQuest, Human Kinetics and Sport England. www.pea.uk.com

Science Museum. www.sciencemuseum.org.uk

Social Exclusion Unit. Includes details of Policy Action Team reports on young people, neighbourhood management, antisocial behaviour, truancy and school exclusion etc., some as full text. www.cabinet-office.gov.uk/seu/index.htm

Sport England. The brand name of the English Sports Council which distributes sports lottery funds. Contains the Sports Gateway database of sports centres, sporting activities, contacts and organisations which can be searched by region., with links to other sites. Provides information on the Activemark Initiate which awards schools for their sports provision. www.sport england.org

Sport Scotland. www.sportscotland.org.uk

Sports Coach UK. www.sportscoachuk.org

Sports Council for Northern Ireland. Sport organisations, youth sport, performance sport etc. www.sportni.org/

Sports Council for Wales. Provides information services of the Welsh Institute of Sport including the Strategy for Welsh Sport; in English and Welsh. www.sports-council-wales.co.uk/

SportsMatch. Government's scheme to encourage commercial sponsorship of grass-roots sport. Administered by Institute of Sport Sponsorship on behalf of Department of Culture, Media and Sport and Sport England. Of interest to sports clubs and organisers, schools, organisers of disabled sport, community groups etc. www.sportsmatch.co.uk

The Home Office. www.homeoffice.gov.uk

UK Sport. Updated weekly, with search facility. Provides overview of UK sport. Includes site map, publications list, and information about UK Sports Institute, ethics and anti-doping, international sports relations, lottery funding, Sport England, World Class Performance Programme, FAQs and links. www.uksport.gov.uk

Wired for Health. Delivers health information and supports National Curriculum. Has links to Mind, Body and Soul site (14–16-year-olds) and LifeBytes (11–14-year-olds). Good A–Z links and sources of information, e.g. asthma, epilepsy, eating disorders, physical activity, special educational needs, smoking. The Healthy Schools Programme contains a downloadable text file of the Government's National Healthy School Standard (1999). www.wiredforhealth.gov.uk

Youth Sport Trust. Registered as a charity in 1994. Its mission is 'to develop and implement, in close partnership with other organisations, quality physical education and sports programmes for all young people, aged 18 months to 18 years in schools and the community'. Includes TOP programme information for early years, primary, secondary, inclusion (for SEN), and Nutella Sports Parent. (See also Institute of Youth Sport Trust above.) www.youth sport.net/yst/index.cfm

Outdoor education sites

Adventure Activities Licensing Authority (AALA). Provides information on the AAL schemes and providers. www.aala.org/
British Orienteering Federation. www.cix.co.uk/%7Ebof/

Women and sport

Islamic Countries' Women's Sport Solidarity Games. Link to 'Women in Iran' webpage. Provides synopsis of History of Islamic Countries' Sports Solidarity Congress for Women, 1991, with excerpts. www.Salamiran.org/women/Olympic/index.html
Sports Illustrated for Women. Interactive US/Canadian site with links to women's sports, scoreboards, events and sports centres. Bi-monthly issues. Current issue available online. www.sports illustrated.cnn.com/womens/
Women's Sports Foundation (WSF). Founded in 1984 to improve and promote opportunities for women and girls in sport. Provides information and news on individual sports (hockey, soccer, weightlifting etc.), and conferences, seminars, exhibitions and awards. www.wsf.org.uk/

Sport for the disabled

British Paralympic Association. Includes information on Sydney, Athens and Beijing. www.paralympics.org.uk/
British Wheelchair Sports Foundation. National organisation for wheelchair sport in the UK. www.bwsf.org.uk

Sports psychology

International Society of Sport Psychology (ISSP). Publishers of the *International Journal of Sport Psychology*. www.issponline.org

Index